Strategic Business Transformation

THE 7 DEADLY SINS TO OVERCOME

Mohan Nair

WILEY

John Wiley & Sons, Inc.

Published by John Wiley & Sons, Inc., Hoboken, New Jersey.

Published simultaneously in Canada.

For general information on our other products and services or for technical support, please contact our Customer Care Department within the United States at (800) 762-2974, outside the United States at (317) 572-3993, or fax (317) 572-4002.

Wiley also publishes its books in a variety of electronic formats. Some content that appears in print may not be available in electronic books. For more information about Wiley products, visit our web site at www.wiley.com.

Library of Congress Cataloging-in-Publication Data:

Nair, Mohan.
  Strategic business transformation : the 7 deadly sins to overcome / Mohan Nair. — 1
      p. cm.
  Includes index.
  ISBN 978-0-470-63222-2 (hardback); ISBN 978-1-118-13443-6 (ebk); ISBN 978-1-118-13444-3 (ebk); ISBN 978-1-118-13445-0 (ebk)
  1. Organizational change.   2. Strategic planning.   3. Success in business.   I. Title.
  HD58.8.N35 2011
  658.4'06—dc23   2011023739

ISBN 978-0-470-63222-2

Printed in the United States of America

10 9 8 7 6 5 4 3 2 1

To Mom, for her endless love and encouragement.

Contents

Preface

Transform. Easier said than done. We used to think that things could stand still, but not any longer. Governments can come and go in short time frames, but as we have seen recently, governments that had withstood multiple attacks can be brought down by a single voice via the Internet. Business is no different.

As the world changes at a rapid pace, some things have not changed—the need for community, the need to create value, the need to serve, and the need to create wealth. Business transformation used to be done once in the life of a business. Now, because of the rapid changes in the fundamental structures that support business, transformation is more frequent to keep up or lead markets.

Even though I had access to technology, this book was handwritten and started on a dinner table in my mother's home far in the South Pacific. I needed to feel the pen in my hand and touch the paper to document the ideas in this book because everything around me is changing and I wanted one thing to remain just for a while. I remember the day I began. It was a great day when I put pen to paper rather than reach for my computer to communicate key messages to whoever would be willing to listen. In times of rapid structural change, we tend to reach for what we find familiar and somewhat everlasting. Business is no different.

The foundational ideas in this book have taken me some time to prepare. The first aspects of these ideas surfaced in the 1990s. The concepts expressed in this book have been implemented successfully in emerging companies as well as in established multi-billion-dollar businesses. In watching these implementations, I have learned they are not as clean as these chapters bound into a book. Rather, these ideas need to be executed well to be successful. In this book, I do not mention any of the companies that have used these methods and instead use other examples as a guide for our learning. By no means does this book imply that the companies mentioned in this book had used or should use these approaches. These companies are admired institutions that reflect the same framework of strategic design and I contend that this framework for strategic business transformation is valuable for your review and understanding.

It began as a book on leadership, but through the years I learned that corporations have two challenges in everything they do—finding leadership and developing strategy. After years of introspective thinking, learning, and corporate experience, I have decided to publish a practical framework for aligning strategy and leadership in the context of transformation.

Strategic Business Transformation is about realizing, responding to, and navigating through a major shift in market need. It is not about strategy but about business design to withstand shifts that break all the foundational understandings of the current market assumptions. Customers migrate to value in transformative markets, and they may not follow the rational rules of the markets of the past.

This book is about finding the correct angle of incidence into the new, forming markets before others realize its existence. When transformation begins in markets, it may be too late to build competencies that you need.

About This Book

To see lasting competitive advantage, we must start with understanding the new principles of transformation; find our core purpose, our cause; refine our understanding of the momentum of the new markets; develop a value proposition that attracts the target customers; build or buy or ally with competencies that produce this value proposition consistently; and form a performance platform so that you can produce this product or service every time, all the time. But to start this, you must have the strategic transformational leaders who have gone through their own change and who can understand and withstand personal and professional transformation because they have seen that service to the greater good is wealth enhancing in our new economy. Peter Drucker, the founder of modern management, stated that the purpose of business is wealth creation. Many have interpreted him to mean make money. I do not. I believe the purpose of business is to create wealth as defined by rational, emotional, and symbolic wealth. Rational wealth is money; emotional wealth is meaning; and symbolic wealth is the participation in something greater than us and in the service of others.

Although respectful of the rational, financial models of transformation, this book argues for the other side to be considered in an organized way. Strategic thinkers tend to be focused, unemotional, and execution focused during transformational times. These are valuable traits. Yet, as observed by Roderick Gilke, Ricardo Caceda, and Clinton Kitts:

> . . . the area of the brain people tend to associate with strategic thought is the prefrontal cortex, known for its role in execution function. It allows humans to engage in anticipation, pattern recognition, probability assessment, risk appraisal and abstract thinking.
>
> However, when we examined the best strategic performers in our sample, we found significantly less neural activity in the prefrontal cortex than in the areas associated with "gut" responses, empathy and emotional intelligence.
>
> "When Emotional Reasoning Trumps IQ,"
> *Harvard Business Review,* September 2010, p. 27

So, leaders have to understand themselves and express their leadership, with service as fuel to actually transform their organization when markets transform. Market transformation can leave some businesses behind while lifting others to new heights. This book is not about specific companies but about the traits and insights that many companies have displayed during market transformation. No one company should be adored or followed for all that it does, but it should be understood for the strategies and the manner in which it performs its work to anticipate transformation and then serve the customers.

Purpose of This Book

In steady-state markets, the knowns dominate the unknowns. The known unknowns can be rationalized into predictable alternative responses. In transforming markets, the unknown unknowns dominate the market changes. The unknown unknowns in markets dominate the knowns. We are seeing structural shifts in markets and these shifts are accelerating transformation. Corporations that want to understand what the anchors are in transformation will find this book helpful.

Another finding in this book is that people have changed in their motivation to work in that they are now more interested in work-life balance, not just work. Many young people want to serve their community and want to work so that they can afford to serve. Corporations that want to engage them cannot appeal just to greed but must also appeal to service and to issues greater than those found in the corporation. People want to serve a good greater than themselves and not perpetuate business for its own survival and growth. They are also tired of imposters in business and will quietly respond to work demands but will not be motivated by the singular pursuit of wealth as motive without a defining principle beyond the work itself. Individuals go home daily to find purpose, and if organizations can integrate that purpose into work they will not be commenting about work-life balance but will be talking about community-job balance. And before we go into believing that all good things do not pay, the future workforce wants to be paid a good wage that grows and also serve the greater good using commercially viable skills and techniques and not just build their muscles at work and build their hearts in nonprofit volunteering. They believe that corporations can put heart and mind in the center of gravity of the activities in the company and find a cause to serve that transcends the day-to-day work. People want purpose at work as well as at home, and they want to integrate both in their day-to-day lives. Also, businesses cannot survive transformation if they focus on responding to wealth accumulation void of purpose and service. We understand this, but in the coming era organizations will not get alignment among the goals, the purpose, and the people without strategic design of the business to address the transformation taking place in the markets and in the individuals who serve these markets.

Essentially, as individual personal transformation is occurring, so is business transformation, and these are interconnected. We are seeing a transformation of principles in our world, and it influences the way wealth is created. Many organizations have found this recipe and have aligned themselves to it. They realize that being authentic is the new way of business, and they push forward for wealth and for purposeful outcomes to communities they serve. They start with creating the conditions where their customers are transformed for the better and they are transformed in service of their cause.

How to Read This Book

Chapter 1 defines Strategic Business Transformation and explains the motivation for such a book. The main focus of this book is the seven issues (or "sins") that have surfaced as the reasons why businesses tend to fail in their attempt to address a transformative shift in the markets they serve. These seven "deadly sins" are addressed in Chapters 3 through 9. These sins can be overcome, not by dealing with them one by one but by considering the recipe of actions that need to be taken to solve them. If worked through, these issues can become the seven "guideposts" for navigating the strategic transformation of markets. Chapter 10 provides examples of people and companies who fit the transformational model.

The book also includes a glossary and section of suggested readings. The glossary is a collection of terms that I use in the book and may be good reference for you.

The chapters build on one another and are best read in serial fashion. The book builds to an understanding of the interrelationships among all the seven sins as a recipe for success, if overcome. These attributes, if aligned, hopefully give an organization the opportunity to anticipate the strategic variables that have yet to surface in a market yet to transform. This book provides a predictive tool and method to identify, understand, and drive to strategic destination while monitoring and managing the present demands of the business.

We Live in Exciting Times

I cannot imagine a more exciting time to be in business. It seems everything we consider anchors in our world has been transformed. We are searching for true north while we navigate through rough waters. However, I get the feeling that we are not trying to get back to where we were but that we want something greater. We have run the races of the past, and they did not make us whole. Now, history may not repeat itself and we have the opportunity to find new ways to find new markets that not just create wealth but create cultures that create wealth. This book is not a philosophical treatment on business but a practical, tested approach of wealth creation. It defines the wealth of an organization in both the explicit financial terms along with the wealth of service to the greater society. In fact, it declares that one will be challenged to create businesses in the next century that have one form of wealth or the other.

For the energy industry, transformation is constant and unpredictable. For the airline industry, things have really changed. What about education? What about health care? What about manufacturing? We are seeing the subtle dismantling of markets not just because the world is flat but because some markets are shrinking, while others are growing; some are going away, while others are being created. For strategists to see through the fog of the future, they must find markers that go beyond the traditional views and see the truth in our future and design their businesses to deliver truth before others can.

Mohan Nair
mohanemerge@gmail.com

Acknowledgments

About 15 years ago, while on my journey to find a new way to understand strategy and leadership, I met with Rajmohan Gandhi, the grandson of Mohandas (yes, I was named after him) Karamchand Gandhi. In that meeting, I was so very excited to have dinner with him and our families. I wondered what to say, what to do, how to act, and so on. We entered the restaurant and before I sat down, in a very polite way, Mr. Gandhi asked me a question. He asked, since I was named after his grandfather, what was I doing to serve mankind? I rushed to tell him of all the boards I was sitting on, all the groups I was associated with, and even ventured to tell him that since I was president of an emerging business that creates jobs, I should justify my service to others. It was at that point that my journey got real. I was not doing anything for society as a whole. I was not building scale to my efforts to create societal wealth and financial wealth for others. Not the scale worthy of dinner conversation with Mr. Gandhi.

I have received many messages from many great minds like this over the years, and so this book is a celebration of the causes that others have taken. Many have helped me through the years, and it is traditional to acknowledge them in this section. I have so many friends and colleagues who have supported me in the creation of this book. I find it humbling to list them all, and it would take a chapter to describe their support and caring for my work. I thank you all for your friendship.

I would like to highlight a few who have been directly associated with the development of this book. I thank my acquisitions editor, Sheck Cho, and development editor, Stacey Rivera, and Chris Gage at John Wiley & Sons for their unique approach in guiding me through the design and delivery of this work.

I want to thank my family for their understanding of my journey through this book. I wrote this book in many places, such as restaurants, Starbucks, and even in my car while I was taking my daughter to her classes. Anushka, you are such a special person and a source of inspiration to me. This book will always remind me of our adventures through life.

I started composing the book at my mother's home, and the chapters gained momentum because it was powered by her sense of service. I know that she is proud to see a book about transformation based on service beyond oneself.

Brad Anderson, former CEO and vice chairman of Best Buy, shared time with me for dinner, and he gave me more insight into the mind of a transformational leader in a few hours than I could have gathered in months. Professor Bala Balachandran, professor at Kellogg School of Management and chairman of Great Lakes University in Chennai, India, has watched me grow these ideas for years, and I appreciate his patience for my journey through ignorance.

I want to also thank Professor Philip Kotler, Kellogg School of Management, for his support of the ideas. Mark Ganz, CEO of Regence, has supported me for several years and embraced the framework many years ago. He had the courage and conviction to lead these ideas into practice as a true servant leader.

I started to write this book in 1992, and it is gratifying to see it finally come to the stage where it is deliverable as a practice, not just a good idea.

I offer this book in the hope that it helps you in building your future and to prove that companies can do good and do well at the same time. I offer this book as a guide to those who understand that to get through structural transformation in markets we must see more than basic strategy and finances but see humanity as customers and find the way to serve their transformation as strategy. Transformation in business depends on our personal transformation. I wish that for you as well.

Strategic Business Transformation

1

Overview

When markets transform, they leave some businesses behind while they lift others to new heights. There may be businesses that survive and grow for longer periods than others, but there is a proven single method that can guarantee continuous and permanent success. However, there are common ingredients that if combined into a unique recipe of capabilities can increase the chances of surviving and growing through a market transformation. This book is about understanding and acting upon strategic market transformations before they arrive, by understanding, anticipating, and designing your business using Strategic Business Transformation principles and techniques. It is about withstanding transformation and leading into it when the traditional anchors we hang on to become incompatible with the new market waves.

No one organization displays all the ingredients of success in a carefully compiled recipe, but many show the key characteristics. Although we all want to rely on the rational research-based analysis, these methods have proven to have limits when the most-studied companies end up failing after the research is published. However, we can explore measures of capability within each of these businesses. Rationale and researching financial models have their place in transformation, but used exclusively without regard to the nonfinancial side of transformation they would present an incomplete picture. The nonfinancial side is about the customer transformation, the value a business can provide that goes beyond competing on the benefits of the product or service provided; it is the opportunity to find new competencies and build a new identity

1

with a market before it transforms. The softer side of transformation is the more challenging and least understood part of business transformation.

Strategic thinkers tend to be focused, unemotional, and distanced, almost as if this gives them more intellectual insight into the work to be done. These are good traits, but any good trait overemphasized becomes unbalanced.

To anticipate, understand, and be on top of lasting, powerful, and insightful market transformation, we must see it in context of a set of key ingredients for successful transformation. I have framed them into "sins to overcome." This book also proposes that the new ways in which business transformation will stick are based on the belief that business transformation will mimic and follow personal transformation. In that context, the principles of strategy transformation must be aligned with the principles of leadership transformation

Leadership is at the heart of everything that is business. Much has been written about the traits of great leaders, and I will draw on this. I will explore a leadership approach that I call Transformational Servant Leadership, which builds on Robert Greenleaf's pioneering concept of servant leadership.[1] Applied to the field of business transformation, transformations both in business and society start in one person who sees the world differently, who transforms himself or herself to reflect on and prepare for this event and then instigates, provokes, and lives this transformation before others do. This spurs others to do the same. Like Gandhi, Mother Teresa, and other social and political heroes, it all starts with one *among* us, and not with one *above* us. Strategic business transformation is not a top-down and trickle-down process. Yet the top-down approach, if modified, can spur lasting transformation in our businesses.

Strategy and Strategic Business Transformation

Strategic business transformation is about developing strategy in anticipation of a dramatic shift in the market, customers, and their desire for products. Since businesses must design their business models to withstand deep change in the markets, what do we use in developing strategy as our "northern star" to guide us when everything around us could be in transition and we have no anchor? Strategic business transformation is not the design of a strategic plan but the design of the business itself to withstand an anticipated transformation of the markets. It must be done before a strategic plan because the plan assumes that a business and its assets exist in some form. Strategy, transformation, and the elements that strategy stands upon are not the same:

- *Strategic Business Transformation.* The design of your business in transformative times, declaring what you stand for, whom you consider the customers to be, and what you do better than others.
- *Strategy.* The pathway to generating revenue and profits and your view of the landscape for the next five years.
- *Strategic Variables.* The elements in the market and your business that, if changed, would trigger a review of your strategy.

Organizations that have not developed a strong understanding of true commitment to their new markets and customer value transition, that do not understand what they believe in and how to express it, that cannot design their authentic talent into competencies, and that cannot outsmart their competitors with a unique offering will probably fail in the long run.

Strategy is about key directions that drive the positioning and actions of the organization. Strategy is about uniqueness and differentiating value to the customers who will pay for it. Usually driven top-down after input is received from all levels of the organization, strategy is about providing a guide to what makes the organization different with measurable, marketable, and manageable activities. A strategic plan should be elegant, understandable, and actionable. Strategy spans many years, sometimes 10 or more, while objectives run for two to three years measured yearly. But in transforming markets, strategy cannot lock itself into the usual incremental views where what is going to happen today will also happen tomorrow. Furthermore, you may have designed your organization in a form that assumes a state of affairs that may not exist after transformation. You must redesign. When markets transform, the standard compass based on a steady-state view cannot guide us through the storm. We must base our direction on our vision and our belief in what the customers will desire and on our view of who we are and what we stand for, more than the mechanics of today's business model and how we are making money today.

Possibly the biggest predictor of failure may be having a current streak of success. The philosophy of "keep doing what we are doing" can sometimes work, but it will not work all the time because markets transform. The hints of transformation come many years earlier, but we tend not to notice because we think we will adapt as it comes, just as incremental change is our friend. When dramatic markets shifts come, companies die, people lose their jobs, and markets do not rebound. Competitiveness flattens, and anyone can make it big if they anticipate, prepare, and launch at the correct time with the right insight.

Why Another Book on Strategy?

This is not another book on strategy but a book about how to anticipate transformation in markets and build your business for advantage ahead of time. This book is about how to navigate markets that are transforming structurally, where the unknown unknowns affect an unpredicted shift in the market and where customers do not know what they will purchase because they are disoriented by market changes. Unknown unknowns are changes that we don't even know exist before they arrive, and when they do, we begin to try to predict their behavior as known unknowns.

John Mackey, cofounder and co-CEO of Whole Foods, expressed it best:

> I can prove that by just saying that nobody Googled anything 13 years ago because Google didn't exist. Nobody had an iPod nine years ago, and nobody had an iPhone five years ago, and nobody was on Facebook seven years ago. The world changes.[2]

Strategy gurus have defined it in so many ways and have contributed so much to strategy development. Here are a few examples of great work that you might want to review:

- Professor Michael Porter's work on competitiveness and strategy[3]
- The late C. K. Prahalad's (and Gary Hamel's) works on core competencies[4]
- Professor Clayton Christensen and his contributions to disruptive innovation technologies[5]

- Renee Mauborgne and W. Chan Kim with their work on Blue Ocean Strategy[6]
- Professor Robert Kaplan and David Norton on Balanced Scorecard[7]

These are but a few of the significant authors of strategy who have helped us form a cohesive understanding of strategy formulation. They are rich with insights and practical approaches to creating, installing, and moving with strategic intent for your organization.

Strategic business transformation is the art and science of understanding which markets are transforming and putting together the framework to review strategy regularly. This process is done before a strategy formulation exercise. It frames the strategic guideposts. It has taken over 15 years to develop, as it has been formed through the learning experiences of several organizations. It is an approach that argues that organizations hold key ingredients to success that if not combined into a recipe, will not withstand market transformation. Organizations can use a lot of the learnings found in the great strategy texts, but what seems yet to be discovered is not which ingredients make up the meal but how to combine the ingredients to create a differentiating meal with a great aftertaste.

Furthermore, with the advent of social networking and the force that comes from the power now given for one to change many, strategic formulation and insight are no longer the territory only of the organization's top leaders. Transforming organizations must master the art of bringing people into the play rather than just handing them a script. These shifts require a new form of strategy formulation and execution that aligns several core aspects of the business.

If Dinosaurs Had Strategy Tools, Would They Have Survived?

Imagine strategic sessions among dinosaurs. Would they have imagined a world without themselves? Could they have used current strategic tools to guide their realization that their world would no longer exist, that the mammals would survive, that small biologically insignificant animals would transform, and that there would be a new form of life that would someday use Facebook? Could they have been guided away from extinction if they had considered that the anchors of their survival would disappear?

Could they have survived using strategic tools available to us today if we advised them? Many organizations have their heads down, assuming that they will be fed for just working hard today. They define the market using their own view of their reality, assuming that the variables that drive their current markets now will drive their future markets. They assume that they are dominant and that the forces that keep them dominant will roam the earth for the next decade.

Tharman Shanmugaratnam, Deputy Prime Minister for the Republic of Singapore, commented at the East Asia World Economic Forum in 2007 that it is not the "known unknowns" but the "unknown unknowns" that we should be concerned about. "Unknown unknowns" was introduced to us in war-gaming decision analysis and project management to refer to events that we cannot predict simply because we did not know they existed before they arrived.

There are the known unknowns we anticipate, but it is the unknown unknowns that will hurt us more. Who predicted the tension in Greek markets, the banking crises, the mortgage crises and the subsequent drop in commercial real estate, or a fight for freedom in Egypt? Who uncovered that the mortgage crises would trigger such a great financial challenge or that the combination of elements created the unemployment in the United States?

Between 2007 and 2010, the following companies were well-regarded businesses, yet they failed:

- American Home Mortgage
- Bombay Company
- CompUSA
- Circuit City
- Lehman Brothers
- Levitz Furniture
- Linens 'n Things
- Mervyns
- Sharper Image
- Wachovia
- Ziff-Davis
- BearingPoint
- Charter Communications
- KB Toys

- Monaco Coach Corporation
- R. H. Donnelley
- Silicon Graphics
- Hollywood Video

The economy can have a significant impact on large and small businesses. The last few years have confirmed that no one is exempt from demise and that transformed markets are not forgiving to any company regardless of its size or market share. For every one of these companies (this is only a sample list), there are others that took market share from them. The false premise would be to chase after those companies and emulate them. However, it is not the company but the mind-set and behavior that we should try to understand.

Predicting Market Transformation

Can we predict which markets are likely to shift in 10 years? Markets are seldom transformed overnight. Just like a good meal on the stove, it takes time for all the ingredients to come together. The conditions for transformation come in and out of the market until they get into a force that triggers transformation. Then transformation accelerates and speeds through the actions and reactions of the market. At this point, markets are in turmoil and predictions become even worse off than before. With multiple variables, it becomes very challenging to formulate the right strategy if you are in the middle of it all. There is so much noise in the system that you cannot formulate the cause and effect of your strategic actions. Just as you cannot formulate strategy while running from a tornado, you cannot predict where it will land. But you can understand the conditions that might create a tornado and plan your strategy around the notion and remain flexible. Meanwhile, some organizations that have been preparing for a transformed market will instigate the transformation or build a timely and prepared response.

80–20 Reversals

Businesses mastered the art and science of predicting their future using advanced models (both financial and customer) because 80 percent of their future was cyclic. What goes up must come down,

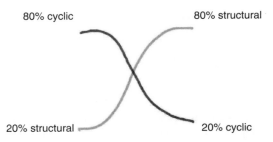

80% cyclic   80% structural

20% structural   20% cyclic

Exhibit 1.1   The Nature of Change Is Changing

while what comes down will go up. Only 20 percent of the market moves were structural, and hence a sudden shift of the market would not likely impact a business' plan. But now, when the unknown unknowns are threatening every variable we have counted on, 80 percent of the variables that shift are structural while 20 percent are predictable (see Exhibit 1.1). We cannot use the strategic data used in the past to find our "true north." Customers may even tell you to stay where you are because they cannot see change coming in their future either (e.g., asking customers whether they would give up their bank teller for an ATM, and they refused to agree to it). Transforming markets have forgotten what got them there and are reforming to the future. We must use new tools and a new approach to understanding the strategic position that we must take by working at a higher altitude in strategy instead of using brute force planning, that is, checking with the markets, figuring the trends, building to customer expectation, and delivering well. Strategic business transformation is about capitalizing upon new principles.

Anticipating Market Transformation

Four key transformation markers are valuable to watch in any market. These markers reveal market vibrations, and at some point the sheer kinetic force of these ingredients tends to drive market shifts that may not return the market to its original dimensions.

Furthermore, the markers are not all needed in transformation, but they may fire in sequence or together. The four markers are:

1. *Is there a trigger to market rethinking value?* Triggers are the forces that make stakeholders rethink the possibilities of change. Skyrocketing prices drive people to consider alternatives.

Deregulation of the markets creates new markets. Increased scrutiny from government or other entities can also start a new force to transformation. We have experienced the gas crises, the financial crises, and the deregulation of the phone companies, and others will come.

2. *Consumers are unaware of the real price and value.* In markets like health care and education, the general public is somewhat unaware of the relationship between price and value. The prices keep going up, and customers seem to be getting less value for what they are paying. Similarly, when prices are subsidized by others or by governments, consumers begin to feel entitled to what they receive. Then value becomes even more distorted. In the education markets, the total cost of education loans has finally exceeded credit card debt in the United States.[8] As of June 2010, Americans owed $826.5 billion in revolving credit while the total for outstanding student loans was $829.785 billion. Currently, the U.S. economic engine is challenged when consumers do not understand value and price equations (i.e., for everything of value there is a corresponding market price). The concept that "there is no free lunch" is still lost in some markets. When prices are subsidized and opaque to the customers, the risk of a revolt to market transformation is high.

3. *Does the market have intermediaries between seller and purchaser?* If this is the case, the value chain can get misunderstood, somewhat misinterpreted, and ripe for optimization of flow and costs. It happened when Walmart created a new way to shop and manage the supply chain. Walmart changed the way manufacturers, brokers, retailers, and wholesalers performed work. It changed the entire business model and activities in the food industry. Knowing what it did well and knowing what its competitors did not know about the consumer brought Walmart to victory with a higher percent margin in the same businesses in which its competitors enjoyed less in margin. The food industry had intermediaries ripe for the picking.

The airline industry has gone through similar transformation. Did you expect this change brought about by the Web? If you had asked focus groups of buyers, they would have told you they would "never" give up on agents because agents helped them deal with the airlines. Banks introduced ATMs despite similar responses from consumers, yet now we like ATMs for convenience and service. When intermediaries try to control access or manage the customer or the seller, the market is ripe for transformative opportunity. What happens when your customers decide that they can take less value for much less price, and you cannot get there for them? Your market may be shifting.

Consider the Honda Civic, which entered the U.S. market in 1972 with Americans laughing at the offering, as big was best in those days. Since Hondas were vulnerable to salt and rust, recalls were extensive. Yet through the years Honda kept developing and improving its cars. When the oil crises brought attention to the more economically attractive cars, Honda stood tall and grabbed share. Value was migrating not from big to small but from big to economical.

Hyundai was positioned for years as a very-low-option offering for many consumers. Slowly but surely, this South Korean car manufacturer is raising its profile in the midrange and high-end markets by appealing to the rational price-conscious (and not status-conscious) purchaser. Hyundai introduced its first car, the Excel, for $5,000 in 1986, when the market was wide open. With steady improvement and sensitivity to where it did not excel, Hyundai is challenging the high-end enthusiasts. Hyundai introduced a 10-year, 100,000-mile warranty to confirm its quality. Since it understood that some buyers would not buy cars because they were afraid of losing their jobs, Hyundai said that it would accept returned vehicles if customers lost their jobs. This presented a new value proposition to the audience: a manufacturer that cared. Approximately 100 cars were returned.[9] Hyundai was initially about being inexpensive, but is quickly moving to being about luxury at a lower price tag. What if it also attacks quality and service? What will its rivals do? What if less expensive and not outdoing the neighbors becomes a virtue, and not showing your wealth or success in a down economy prevails?

4. *Are the leaders in the industry perceived to be enjoying too much success while clients are suffering?* If so, transformation, or at least disruption, is approaching. In some cases, the executives may not be enjoying themselves, but it may be perceived

this way. Some markets, like entertainment and sports, do not suffer from this predicament.

If lower-cost, highly efficient disruptors are roaming around, they prepare the market for transformation by introducing rapidly evolving disruptive solutions. Priceline.com and Expedia.com transformed the booking space of the airline industry, while online brokerage firms like Charles Schwab brought new personality to discount brokerages. Amazon.com transformed the world of bookstores, and iTunes changed the music world on the shoulders of Napster, which pioneered the approach. Is industry "data obese" but "knowledge starved" while the customers and buyers want wisdom?

Exhibit 1.2 illustrates some of the industries that fall into this assessment.

During World War II, British forces in Singapore focused all their defenses and artillery toward the sea to the south to guard against attacks from the Japanese forces. Believing that their enemy

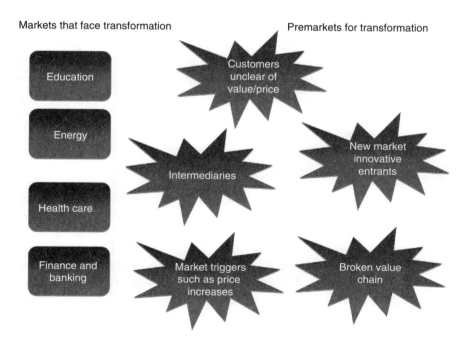

Markets that face transformation

Premarkets for transformation

Education

Energy

Health care

Finance and banking

Customers unclear of value/price

Intermediaries

New market innovative entrants

Market triggers such as price increases

Broken value chain

Exhibit 1.2   Industries in Transformation

would attack from the South China Sea, the British were imbalanced in their strategy. Singapore is connected to the Malayan peninsula to the north via a small, three-quarter-of-a-mile causeway. The Japanese forces, after careful consideration, walked into Singapore via this causeway to capture Singapore.

Many times, strategy and the associated tactics depend on the organizational worldview and assumptions. If the view of the business does not adjust, morph, or transform, the organizations become overrun with challengers who have identified their strategy toward a transformed world. Just as the Japanese were seeking a transformed world, their approach was also transformative and unpredictable to the British.

This story reminds me that the Japanese forces lost the battle in the long run for the very reasons that they won in Singapore. They did not transform as markets transformed; they tried to force their worldview onto a transforming world. The British encountered the same challenge as their worldview imposed on India was also overturned, not by an army but by a single concept found in a single person—Mohandas Gandhi. The worldview of successful organizations seems to reward the market truth that has changed and adapted. History is filled with stories that show losses for the side that does not transform because leaders failed to see a transformation about to happen and led their teams into difficulties. In this sense, leaders must first transform their view of the world before they can lead the team. This transformation is critical to the strategic business transformation proposed in this book and will be explored in detail in Chapter 5.

What Is Strategic Business Transformation?

Remember travel agents? Where did they go? How about the banker who visits you? The mainframe computer? Film-based cameras? The typewriter? The vinyl record, or the CD for that matter? All these markets transformed in our lifetime. I remember when I waited in line in Orchard theatre in Singapore to witness and experience the first escalator. I remember the first television we had in our home. The neighbors would crowd outside our windows to watch it with us. And what about the laptop? Will the idea of a large disk on a laptop sustain itself despite cloud-based storage?

Either organizations transform markets or markets transform organizations. When small changes in a market start to change the customer model, the financial model, and/or the business model, then organizations must transform with it or go extinct in the long run. When we speak of transformation strategies, we must have a view of the following transformations, which are a result of the changes we can expect. Namely, the customer's needs and interests change, the financial model for how you make money may change, and the market may shift:

- Customer model—what customers buy consistently, how they buy, when they consider and what they consider value for a price.
- Financial model—the profit and loss framework of the organization. How is the money that funds the actions of the organization made? How is revenue allocated, and how does money flow as the bloodstream of the business? How is cost allocated, and how are decisions made from this allocation?
- Market model—product, price, promotion/brand, and channels. How are these measured and managed? What are the key business processes, and how do they differentiate the business?

Transformation is different from change in that change is about knowing where the puck is going and predicting positions of the market, while transformation is about finding new arenas with different elements of your assets in a different combination. Change is about predicting and responding to business cycles, and transformation is about finding the new normal. Sometimes markets make structural shifts that make predictions almost impossible. In this situation, market transformations will confuse many of the players. How do you know the organization's new strategy has the best possibility of success? Let us look at the core differences between change and transformation:

Change is:

- Cyclic.
- 80 percent regression, 20 percent structural.
- What goes up will come down.

- An adjustment in volume.
- Knowing where the market is going.
- Incremental changes in product and service design.
- Speed to market or good response works.

Transformation is:

- Structural shift in how the market works.
- 80 percent structural, 20 percent regression.
- What goes down may stay down.
- A correction or movement to the new market.
- The market is leaving; new markets form.
- Innovation is welcomed in product and service design.
- New business models are welcomed.
- New responses to the existing market and new markets are welcomed.

Transformation is seldom about sudden change, but it may seem that way because several unnoticed changes may happen all at once.

Who could have predicted that Greece would challenge the financial balance of the European markets, creating a ripple effect that would challenge even the U.S. markets?

Toyota was challenged with apparent brake failures and with a brand declaration "moving forward." An oil spill devastated the southern coastline of the United States. Earlier, Thailand suffered from a coup. All this may seem unpredictable. Businesses can build their futures without anchoring their business model on such events but on anchors that never change because they are based on human behavior and principles rather than market dynamics. Are these changes transformational? Are these shifts tectonic, where the market is restructuring how it wants to be served, or is everything just trends? Add to this the transformation of how people communicate using social media. The information flowing between nations, individuals, and organizations shows no sign of slowing down. Gregg Easterbrook says:

> The ancient Greeks had considerable knowledge, though compared to us, little information. For instance, the Greeks believed matter was made from four elements: the latest count is 119. Today's typical American high school student has at his

or her disposal more facts about science, biology, geography, physics and astronomy than was known to all Greek thinkers combined.

. . . but when information changes from a stream (the Greeks) to a river (the present) to Niagara Falls (the new future), how will we ever slow down enough to achieve knowledge?[10]

Importance of the Transformation Effect

There are three reasons why businesses must watch the transformation effect:

1. We experienced a downturn in 2007 during the banking system crises. The housing bubble burst, and unemployment reached 9.8 percent in November 2010.[11] The results of this downturn have been unprecedentedly transformative as forces gaining momentum in the markets will be felt for years to come. Consumers were not spending, and businesses were not borrowing. The fuel of our economy is spending, and this is not growing even though we see positive signs of consumer purchasing goods at year end. Stock market reactions reduced retirement nest eggs, and retirees understand that they have to keep working.
2. Government has decided to engage in the business of business because it believes that businesses are failing the community at large. Now the government is competing and controlling the market dynamics for fear of market failure, and the free-market dynamics seem not to be trusted.
3. Consumers are rethinking their lifestyle and purchases, and so are businesses, which like to hold onto cash in reserve. They are holding on to investments. Maybe we will go back to the spending days of the past as the economy gets better, but since the last downturn, many average consumers are concerned about the future and hesitant about returning for more than financial reasons. They are witnessing a changing world of priorities and are questioning greed as a virtue.

Transformation does not take place once every 10 years but when markets warn you that the strategic variables you used to define your strategy have been replaced. According to Vinay Leuto, Frank Ribeiro, and Andrew Tippens, "To navigate such a rocky landscape, companies must be ready to repeatedly transform themselves—indeed, to institutionalize the capacity to alter strategies again and again—as business conditions require."[12] They confirm that the problem is that most companies do not have "an adequately proactive roadmap of transformation."

Markets in Transformation Are Re-creating Themselves

W. Chan Kim and Renee Mauborgne, authors of *Blue Ocean Strategy*, describe markets as expanding. Unlike battle, where most of our business analogies come from, they state:

> Unlike war, however, history of industry shows us that the market universe has never been constant; rather blue oceans have continuously been created over time. To focus on the red ocean is therefore to accept the key constraining factors of war—limited terrain and the need to beat an enemy to succeed—and to deny the distinct strength of the business world: the capacity to create new market space that is uncontested.[13]

They contend that when markets expand, so does our opportunity to capture "blue oceans" rather than stay only in the "red ocean." Strategic business transformation is about finding those latent opportunities in the ever-expanding market. They continue:

> . . . history shows that industries are constantly being created and expanded over time and that industry conditions and boundaries are not given; individual actors can shape them.

Given that the business opportunity universe expands and contracts over time, what are the ways we can view, diagnose, predict, and identify opportunities? How do we understand not just the trends everyone identifies within a market but also the future momentum that creates new markets?

When Apple introduced the iPad, it revolutionized an existing market of tablet PCs. Just as Apple took the mp3 market to new heights with the iPod, and the phone market with the iPhone, its iPad is now finding uses in expanding markets. Children use it, teachers use it, and doctors use it.

Summary and Observations

If you run a business in an industry that is shifting structurally and you believe that the customers will change, or if you want change because you have found a cause that will enable your company to transform the industry, then you must prepare for this transformation. You should put together a way to view the future and a way to diagnose which variables to watch and which to ignore. How do you find a guiding star when the sky is filled with clouds? Chapters 2 through 9 outline seven attributes to understand, watch, and avoid. I call them "the seven deadly sins" because following them increases the likelihood that your business will be swept away in the coming storms.

These seven are best overcome by turning them into ingredients for success, putting them together and aligning one with the other to create the foundation for an effective strategic direction. They are best deployed in anticipation of a transforming market. In transformation, too much noise is introduced into the system, and one cannot find the key signals that give direction. So it is best to start early, watch for the real signals, and formulate your organization direction. The seven sins provide the warning signs to watch for these signals that will guide us through the noise. Organizations lose their identity before they lose their way. This is about gaining and discovering your organization's identity, and then your direction.

Notes

1   Greenleaf: Center for Servant Leadership. www.greenleaf.org.
2   Justin Fox, "What Is It That Only I Can Do?" *Harvard Business Review* interview with John Mackey (January–February 2011), pp. 119–123.
3   Michael E. Porter, "What is Strategy?" *Harvard Business Review* (November–December 1996).
4   C. K. Prahalad and Gary Hamel, *Competing for the Future* (Boston: Harvard Business Press, 1996).
5   Clayton M. Christensen, *The Innovator's Dilemma: When New Technologies Cause Great Firms to Fail* (Boston: Harvard Business Press, 1997).

6   W. Chan Kim and Renee Mauborgne, *Blue Ocean Strategy: How to Create Uncontested Market Space and Make Competition Irrelevant* (Boston: Harvard Business Press, 2005).

7   Robert S. Kaplan and David P. Norton, *The Balanced Scorecard: Translating Strategy into Action* (Boston: Harvard Business Press, 1996).

8   Mary Pilon, "Student-Loan Debt Surpasses Credit Cards," *Wall Street Journal,* August 9, 2010, http://blogs.wsj.com/economics/2010/08/09/student-loan-debt-surpasses-credit-cards/

9   "Hyundai: Driven to Success," February 28, 2010, www.cbsnews.com.

10   Gregg Easterbrook, *Sonic Boom: Guide to Surviving and Thriving in the New Global Economy* (New York: Random House, 2011), p. 67.

11   United States Department of Labor Statistics, www.bls.gov/cps/.

12   Vinay Leuto, Frank Ribeiro, and Andrew Tippens, "It Makes Sense to Adjust," *Strategy and Business,* Issue 59 (Summer 2010), p. 12.

13   W. Chan Kim and Renee Mauborgne, *Blue Ocean Strategy* (Boston: Harvard Business Press, 2005), p. 6.

CHAPTER

2

Strategic Business Transformation:
Seven Sins to Overcome

W hat do Les Schwab (a multi-billion-dollar tire company), Best Buy (the largest electronics retailer), Starbucks (the world's most-well-known coffee company), and Southwest Airlines (an upstart airline) have in common with great transformational leaders like Mahatma Gandhi, Martin Luther King Jr., and Mother Teresa?

They all transformed markets and created enterprises; they had transformational leaders who found their voice through the organization; they did it by first uncovering their true self-purpose, their footprint in the world, and found a purpose greater than themselves. They executed on their strategy with focus and dominated their market category. They understood that strategy is the building block of a brand and they created long-lasting identity in markets that resisted ideas such as theirs. They all created movements, not motion. They did this by defining a concept and putting that philosophy and concept into practice in person. They transformed the world by first transforming themselves and then impacted an entire market. They also understood that building an enterprise is one half of the solution and that building a community is the other half. Corporations that understand that their role is not just wealth creation but also community enhancement, beyond philanthropy, are the next-generation transformational organizations. But we should guard against admiring specific corporations because each has their own recipe for success and emulating the successful ones will not suffice:

> If there is no perpetually high-performing company and if the same company can be brilliant at one moment and wrong-headed at another; it appears that the company is not the appropriate unit of analysis in exploring the roots of high performance and blue oceans.[1]

Through their research, W. Chan Kim and Renee Mauborgne declare that it is the strategic move, not companies or the industry, that is the right "unit of analysis" for explaining high performance and creating new markets (i.e., blue oceans).

The patterns they professed in their groundbreaking research in *Blue Ocean Strategy* reinforce the message in this book. Yet, the unique contribution found in Strategic Business Transformation is in the corelationship between transformed leaders who transform themselves and their world and transformed businesses that transform their markets. It is one thing to find new markets and inhabit them; it is another to transform yourself as an organization for the sake of transforming your customers who look to you and then transform or create new markets as a result. This corelationship is the power source for strategic market moves in the next millennium. Furthermore, strategic business transformation starts with being the change you wish to see first rather than driving a strategy that maintains a servant leadership model inside and a market-conquering model outside. We tell our teams to care for each other but to kill and destroy others outside. This duality is failing business today.

It is also about technique and competence in aligning the key attributes of market transformation to the solutions the company offers and to create markets by re-creating the company's capability to serve and not attack markets.

Strategic moves are made only after strategic insights are gathered. This idea, concept, vision, or sight of the mind is the core premise of strategic business transformation. We always witness coffee drinking in restaurants; we saw couches in tea houses; we knew of baristas for coffee but we never really gathered the insight to serve people by trained baristas who could engage consumers creating an atmosphere that seems like an extension of their living rooms. Howard Schultz did. Just as Gandhi built a movement and a platform for transformation on a message that transformed the world, businesses can build profits and growth on a message in transforming markets. Organizations that capture these strategic insights are the foundation of business transformation. There is a great deal of corelationship between transformed leaders and transformational companies. There are patterns in both organizations and leaders that relate and can be studied for business transformation. In the previous market dynamics of status quo, trending the past is the basis for understanding the future. In transformation, there is no past except as it plays out for the future. In organizational history, what you have built as a capacity or capability is surely used in the future. In transforming markets, not all capabilities transport to the future because the future is based off other variables.

This book identifies several exemplary companies as benchmarks of successful transformative thinking and action, which started from one person in an organization and blossomed out to the customers—from the inside out. I do not argue that these companies should be admired or emulated, because what is important is not the ingredients of their success more than how they used the same ingredients that other companies had but found their recipe with an eye to a greater transformation of their new and existing customers.

The other important point is that these companies focused through the vision of their CEOs, or those who rose to be CEOs, to focus not on their own company's transformation but the transformation of their customers. They were all powered by what they believed their customers or prospects deserved as change. They wanted a betterment of their customers first and this powered their search for truth in their offerings.

So what is the unit of analysis in exploring the roots of high performance or new market discovery? This book argues that the seven elements that I call "sins" of business transformation if overcome and mastered can assemble the recipe for the roots for transformational potency.

According to Blue Ocean Strategy, both *Built to Last* and *In Search of Excellence*[2] founded their beliefs on high-performance organizations as the unit of analysis. As time passed, these organizations did not continue their leadership trends. These books serve a strong basis selecting the elements within these organizations that can make successful transformations. Focusing on the habits of successful organizations might be misplaced, because "much of the success attributed to some of the model companies in *Built to Last* was the result of industry sector performance rather than the companies themselves."[3]

However, Strategic Business Transformation is not about which companies or habits rise to the top. It is a recipe of contributive elements that if missing or underused could cause failure as organizations attempt to maneuver through a transformative market shift.

The seven ingredients of the premise are:

1. Ignoring the new principles of business transformation (see Chapter 3)
2. Driving without a "cause" (see Chapter 4)
3. Missing market momentum (see Chapter 5)
4. Ignoring the two orders of value (see Chapter 6)
5. Overlooking transformational servant leadership (see Chapter 7)
6. Mistaking capability for strategic competence (see Chapter 8)
7. Expecting flawless execution without a performance platform (see Chapter 9)

Let us touch on each of the opportunities for improvement and then the chapters that follow will drive details.

Ignoring the New Principles of Business Transformation

The new principles of transformation are based on a fundamental premise that companies lose their identity before they lose their way in transformation. Many companies that fail focus on the outward manipulation of markets and customers driven from the "ego" of the organization. What powers your organization's insight into the new markets is best found in the need to serve a larger good than just internal needs of wealth creation. Although some say that when there is no money, there is no mission, others believe that if there is no mission, there will be no money. This is because markets are sensitive to purposeless wealth creation and no amount of donations to needy organizations at year end will solve a brand problem founded on the lack of organizational introspection on purpose and value. The new principles relate that in order to transform, organizations must first understand that:

- To change the world, they must first change their organization.
- To transform the organization, they must transform their communities of employees, and to do so is to transform each and every employee.
- "It is not about you" but about you in the greater good of community that strategy is focused on. The bull's-eye is not the company and its profits but the customer and their family.
- One idea can change all ideas, and that one person among us can change all of us with one powerful idea.
- Knowing the difference between transformation and change is critical for transformation to last.
- Keeping score is important but keeping direction with score is more important.
- Truth is the ultimate organizer not money.
- Looking at the prize while aiming at the target is a sure way to miss the target.

These principles can be incorporated in the organization's operating principles or just used to set the table for transformation recipe. Levi Strauss & Co. lives its principles and has kept its core values throughout its transitions. In fact, its values sustain its profits: "Performance and great values reinforce one another and create a virtuous circle. We call this 'profits through principles.'"[4]

Driving without a Cause

Mission, visions, value, and the like seem compulsory in all organizations. Yet many employees cannot remember them; they don't believe them and never use them. Strategic business transformation in markets and in self cannot function without purpose. The leaders that uncovered their purpose drove and built markets. Once organizations know why they exist and to whom they want transformation to happen for and why, they are often changed with the conviction which brings an audacity and authenticity to make the world view happen. Discovering a cause greater than any one employee and greater than the whole propels organizations beyond the speed of lofty, purposeless, or narcissistic goals. Phrases such as "it's not about you" remind us that what motivates and propels organizations to inhabit a cause must be uncovered, else we respond to transformation and not generate it.

Missing Market Momentum

New markets can be created during transformation. Traditionally, products seek customers; customers form markets; and markets move with momentum. In transformation principle, momentum is identified before anything else; customers and prospects respond to momentum; then products respond to serve these prospects to move with purposeful intent. If organizations respond to markets they do not lead in its creation and will not define them. In transformation, finding markets that others have created can be valuable if you can do it better, faster, cheaper, and be a fast follower. However, it might be best if you understood the momentum that drives these markets and serve them well with little to no regard about the argument that it is either best to follow or lead. Both are bad options if you do it wrong.

Ignoring the Two Orders of Value

"Southwest Airlines created a blue ocean by breaking the tradeoffs customers had to make between the speed of airplanes and the economy and flexibility of car transport," says W. Chan Kim and Renee Mauborgne:

> By eliminating and reducing certain features of competition and raising others in the traditional airline industry, as well as by creating new factors drawn from the alternative industry of car transport, Southwest Airlines was able to offer unprecedented utility for air travelers and achieved a lead in value with a low-end business model.[5]

These elaborations show how to understand the new market segment before it arrives. Southwest Airlines first offered service to the high-flying executive. In fact, its advertisements early on spoke of point-to-point flight with flight attendants wearing "hot pants."

It was called the love airline before the low-cost airline tag appeared. Southwest noted the migration of customers and transformed its asset to a new market available to it. It applied its capabilities to the customers who migrated in their sense of value and created a new evolving market—the low-cost flyer who values on-time departures. That used to be your and my grandmother. This is a market that is expanding into business travelers who are tired of the larger airlines, which treat them with less value as more and more people are exclusive.

Value is an overused word because beauty is in the eye of the beholder. However, organizations that do not understand how to transfer and connect the market movement and momentum into value to the customers that emerge from a transformation will fail to gain share and succeed. Two dimensions are discussed. One is the dimension heard most (i.e., emotional and rational value propositions). Here, customers will purchase your product or service because, for example, they like the benefits of such a purchase. You purchase a car for safety, speed, and so on. The emotional element is that you purchase the car because it makes you feel powerful or cute or upscale. There is another dimension rarely discussed called the "higher order" value proposition. This higher order is usually hidden and is more an expression of what you believe and how you want to bring others to the table and less you. High-order value proposition is why Martin Luther King Jr. had fans and followers. He stood where others did not, and they wanted him symbolically. If it was only emotional value to stand in front of the police, they would have run more than stayed. They stayed and marched because of the higher-order value of representing the generations to follow, the ethics of it all, and the belief in things greater than just "me."

Value is also about understanding your target customers. Before Starbucks formed the new market of coffee-obsessed buyers, many customers knew how to make or buy coffee. Things changed, and a new format for coffee purchase entered with Starbucks. Now customers pay significant prices for the experience, and they visit often. Before Les Schwab placed tires in the retail stores so that customers could browse the tires before purchase, no one really wanted that to be a value offer. Before Best Buy took away commissions for its sales people, sales people and commissions were synonymous. Value propositions do not exist in isolation and must be related to customer value both in the high- and low-order dimensions. In transformation, one must understand and inhabit the needs and wants of the customer who is transforming and forming a newly approached market.

Overlooking Transformational Servant Leadership

Leadership is the underpinning of all transformations in markets. The principles of hard-driving, greedy, narcissistic leaders have faded in value. It is now time for companies who have leaders who believe in something greater than themselves. Talent is attracted to these companies because they have seen and experienced the short-comings of uncontrolled greed. The talent pool is transforming to find meaning in work and life. When they see that selling their souls along with the product they market or build is necessary for keeping the job, they are starting to devalue work all together and are start-ing to resign away their days to putting time in rather than purposefully execute the job for the sake of others. People are turning to meaningful work with meaningful business models based on their own desire to feel fulfillment. Leadership of this kind is transformational servant leadership.

Servant leadership, defined by Robert K. Greenleaf, has become the approach many businesses are taking in defining a new form of leadership based on service rather than hierarchical controls. Servant leadership, according to Greenleaf, is about service first and leaders' drive second versus leadership drive first and service second. A detailed description of this is found in www.greenleaf.org/whatissl/. Transformational servant leadership builds on the concepts of service but places emphasis on self-transformation prior to organi-zational transformation. In other words, leaders change themselves before they can have impact on the individuals in corporations. Furthermore, it is the focus on service that transforms them and their skills. Because their focus is greater than themselves and not so self-directed, they begin to change others. Leadership needed for transformative environments is different than other leadership models. Gandhi, the Mahatma, transformed an entire nation and the worldview while he built a strong following of socially responsi-ble leaders to free India from British rule. Gandhi was not only a soulful leader; he also was an economist, a lawyer with strong entre-preneurial tendencies. He built an everlasting brand and destroyed the brand of the British leadership even though the British was based on intellectual superiority and might. His journey is the journey of a transformative leader. But how does this apply to business? Business is merely a false unit of exclusion from such leadership and in fact, if we had more Gandhis in this business world, we might see the business world in a different way. We tend to see the transformative business leaders differently from the social reformers like Gandhi and Mother Teresa, but they were business people too. This is the delusion that separates us from learning about transformations through the eyes of true social entrepreneurs.

In Chapter 7, we will review and describe how transformational servant leaders function. We will study how transformational servant leaders come to be that way and how it differs from traditional leadership perspectives. We should allow for social reformers to be viewed as entrepreneurs. We should reclassify them as business icons as well as leaders who should be allowed to earn top dollars in their quests to bring an enterprise into the economy. "But the greatest leaders who exercise transformational leadership are those who combine brains, heart, and soul," says Klaus Schwab, founder of the World Economic Forum. He continues:

> A leader's professionalism breeds respect in others, and so his brains are essential. But there must be a harmonic relationship between brains and heart. These leaders' belief in what they are doing unlocks the drive and creativity needed to succeed.[6]

Leaders of corporations can earn dollars and also dedicate their lives to building companies that transform society while creating profits for our world economies. Why not?

Mistaking Capability for Strategic Competence

Most times what we see as competency is what an organization does well or better than others. This is viewed as the unchangeable. Capabilities are what your organization has the ability to do for customers. Competence is the unique recipe of your offering expressed by the activities within your organization and your partners that provide a defensible expression of what you stand for. Trader Joe's has gained loyal customers because they are capable in selling you good produce and groceries. But they are competent in driving their belief systems about conservation, their shop experience, and their community spirit. You can almost picture that their shoppers roam the rainforest to provide you food in a sustainable way.

But nowadays, what you are good at may not be of value and might have to morph. Furthermore, in the past, competencies are usually what you can "do," not what you stand for and how you express it. In transformation, markets and customers look to believe in something and someone.

Hence, two orders of competency emerge in organizations. The first is the low-order competency, which is usually highly developed, and the second is high-order competency, which is usually less developed and understood. The low order is viewed as the activities the organization combines to offer as product or service that customers purchase. The high order is viewed as the way the organization expresses what they believe and how customers are the purpose behind that belief. These competencies seldom change, while the low order can change regularly. Starbucks is about good coffee and about community. Yet, Starbucks is also about people in the high order, and everything Starbucks does seems to reflect its respect for the individual identity and expression. United Services Automobile Association (USAA) is about the war fighter and everything they stand for. But their low order is about efficient selling and marketing of products pioneering the direct marketing channels.

What if your organization lacks the competencies of the transformed markets? What do you do? What rules of engagement do you follow to gain this insight and the talent necessary to win? This is outlined in the chapters under the topic of competency gathering. Reactive organizations run from one acquisition with high prices and move to the next. They stumble from realizing they are late to market and purchase or merge in the hopes of finding the secret to market dominance. Transformative organizations align with partners through four approaches:

1. *Build:* Do it yourself.
2. *Buy:* Acquire talent as well as capability.
3. *Borrow:* Work as partners.
4. *Bury:* Define the market so that the competitive ideas are nullified.

Expecting Flawless Execution without a Performance Platform

Organizations tend to adopt new techniques to improve execution by bringing experts in or sending experts out to learn and then implement. After years of change-management programs, companies are change fatigued. They are tired and cynical of yet another way to be competitive. Many times, more and more is asked of the organization without a context for employees and customers to frame improvement initiatives. Furthermore, if you were to ask organizations' executives what their platform for excellence is, what would you discover? Most of the time, it would not be clearly definable; sometimes it would be purely operational like manufacturing techniques; many times it would be proven methods like activity-based cost management or six sigma for efficiencies. What about data and information? Is it valuable to business? The answer is absolutely yes, but if asked what their data and information personality is, the executives would question the terms. They may have a strategy for data and information but they may be challenged to discuss how information and data is used in the company and why.

Transformative organizations master the creation of a performance platform. They can assess the value of new methods and ideas on that platform, which they use to reject or accept methods that are like applications on the iPad. Corporations that want to find their winning way through transformation know that execution is the cornerstone of strategy and that a performance platform gives them security like the hull of a ship.

Seven Sins as a Framework for Strategic Business Transformation

Exhibit 2.1 illustrates the key elements of a transformation framework, which we will walk through in this book. It is in these sectors of the illustration that breakdown occurs when one piece does not relate, connect, or align with the other. We will explore each of these elements as ingredients to success under the framework of the sins to avoid. Remember that the recipe of these combined is more important than the exactness and specificity of each ingredient in the mix.

Summary and Observations

The following are seven areas on which to focus strategic business transformation to design our new business:

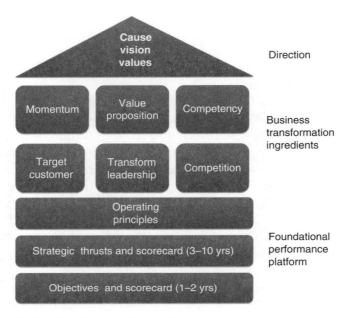

Exhibit 2.1   Business Transformation Framework

1. Ignoring the new principles of business transformation
2. Driving without a cause
3. Missing market momentum
4. Ignoring the two orders of value
5. Overlooking transformational servant leadership
6. Mistaking capability for competence
7. Expecting flawless execution without a performance platform

If you decide to build a transformation plan for your organization and follow these guideposts, it is important to note that it is not the following of these guides that makes you successful in leading through a transformation of your market. It is about combining all the talent, the technology, and the tools in your organization into the right recipe that can make the difference.

Notes

1   W. Chan Kim and Renee Mauborgne, *Blue Ocean Strategy: How to Create Uncontested Market Space and Make Competition Irrelevant* (Boston: Harvard Business Press, 2005), p. 10.

2 Larry Wasserman and Tom Peters, *In Search of Excellence*, (New York: Warner Books, 1982), Jim C. Collins and Jerry Porras, *Built to Last: Successful Habits of Visionary Companies* (New York: Harper Business Essentials).

3 W. Chan Kim and Renee Mauborgne, *Blue Ocean Strategy*, (Boston: Harvard Business Press, 2005), p. 9. Reference on Richard Foster and Sarah Kaplan book, *Creative Destruction* (New York: Doubleday, 2001).

4 Marc Benioff, *The Business of Changing the World: Twenty Great Leaders on Strategic Corporate Philanthropy* (New York: McGraw-Hill, 2007), p. 90.

5 W. Chan Kim and Renee Mauborgne, *Blue Ocean Strategy* (Boston: Harvard Business Press, 2005), p. 38.

6 Marc Benioff, *The Business of Changing the World: Twenty Great Leaders on Strategic Corporate Philanthropy* (New York: McGraw-Hill, 2007), p. 241.

3

Sin #1: Ignoring the New Principles of Business Transformation

Businesses must adapt to changing and transforming markets and to consumers' changing needs and behaviors. Everything should be on the table when change and transformation are on the horizon. Many organizations struggle with change and align it to the challenge of transforming a culture because they believe that culture is the underpinning element of change. Culture is one part of the equation to solve transformation but the alignment is strategy and leadership. People in an organization will not change just to change but will focus their attention on a purpose that the organization expects.

Business tends to separate leadership and strategy in ways that inhibit growth and transformation. For example, leadership is viewed as a skill set gained through experience rather than an act of service (i.e., servant leadership). Also, leadership principles are separated from strategic principles. Hence, we speak of service to our employees and leadership in terms of how we should care for them, but our language to articulate strategy speaks of conquering markets, killing the competition, and capturing customers, but internal culture basically destroys that belief system. It is fundamentally misaligned and obviously unmanageable in the trenches. When corporations exhibit a way to behave to our customers but mistreat their own employees, they will not win customers in the long term because customers will know. Also, when corporations do not link strategy with leadership, they may miss out on the new principles of business transformation which are based on the principles of personal transformation.

Many young people are inclined to build companies that not only generate revenue and profit but also support the needs of society. The idea of separating philanthropic endeavors from business goals seems alien to them. We tend to expect that philanthropy must be defined by financial sacrifice on the part of the business that drives for this. But a new group of thinkers and doers are forming an evolved business model that asserts that you can make money while serving society. In fact, if you think of making money without thinking of the greater contributions to society, you will neither attract the right people nor make money in the long run.

Strategy and leadership principles are actually one and the same. They are expressions of a core philosophy of purpose that an organization commits to. Therefore, the older models of transformation inflict change upon others both as individuals and also as corporations upon other corporations or markets. These rules are fast becoming obsolete because the people who are the basic objects of change and transformation are also transforming in the way they are motivated and evolving. They need much more than inflictions of change from the outside in; they seek transformation from within. They need inspiration to lead through a strategy that aligns with not just what to get done but how strategy gets accomplished.

Aligning Transformational Leadership with Corporate Strategy

Where do servant leadership and corporate strategy meet? What does servant leadership manifestation look like in corporations when it relates to strategy rather than leadership? How do we know when all or many of the elements within the philosophy of servant leadership express themselves in and through an institution?

Corporations tend to view leadership as a way to lead rather than a way a business needs to exist and grow. To move beyond the accepted territories of leadership style to the way a corporation wins markets and develops customer relationships, we must consider the ways in which transformational leadership principles serve strategy.

This chapter explores a form of leadership that is inspiring to others and also designed into the business framework within the front end of a corporation (i.e., in its strategic expression and voice).

The essence of this chapter lies in the belief that:

- Strategy is an expression of an organization's true core belief in action.
- Transformational leadership style and philosophy must not be relegated to how we lead internally in the corporation but must also be applied to how we build and express the brand and the strategy.
- Hence, how we behave with one another and ourselves is the basis for how we imagine and execute our strategy.

Speaking of transformational leadership and strategy . . . the language of transformational leadership expresses ideas in the form of an inward journey to discovery, passion, patience and empowerment, listening, and, most of all, self-transformation.

The language of strategy expresses itself as competitive forces, winning market share, destroying the competition, defining and measuring value propositions and brand equity, shareholder value, and wealth creation.

Is there a common language for these two foundations to dialog? But before we explore this language and the form in which both can exist, a few further complications need some attention. One is about making strategy a process and not an insight-generating activity; the second is about working on the wrong foundation when you make strategy formulation the actions of the elite and expect the others to lead after.

Complication #1: Mistaking the Process and Output for Real Outcomes

In the rawest of definitions, strategy design and development, just like leadership design and development, can degrade into the belief that the generally acceptable processes will derive outputs. If we just follow the process, we will gain insight. Many corporate executives go through their summers defining frameworks for strategy development with large amounts of input in the form of competitive intelligence, market analysis, and customer intelligence. They use a regular process surrounded by a corporate retreat environment behaving like yogis who leave the "real" world to gain insight. They return with their own tablets of thought, while only a few roads away their competitors do the same with their own sets of inputs.

This method can give you "eyesight" into the industry you serve, foresight as you predict the directions the market can take, and true insight into who are the new customers in a transformed market and what they truly want and will pay for because they value your value proposition as different and compelling as they are themselves transforming. This is the challenge of any transforming company. Insight is a rare commodity, and no process in the world can guarantee this output consistently.

Herb Kelleher, chairman emeritus and former CEO of Southwest Airlines, put it clearly:

> Over the years we have developed not only a different strategy but also a different strategic planning process. Basically, we just don't do it![1]

Complication #2: When Employees Feel Entitled to Watch and Not Lead

Meanwhile, the employees, who are mostly left out, await this insight to fall upon them after the summer ends. Discussions evolve as to how to get others committed to the strategy that only a few own. Without insight and only process to hold on to, the senior executives have no inspiration and just output to deliver to the waiting employees. Many forget that employees, like customers, understand the difference between commitment and agreement—motivated service (i.e., actually act on the information). So employees undergo the process but never really offer their leadership at work because they see no insight in progressive improvements. They see the mundane wrapped in process.

As Greenleaf declares, "The best knowledge is not certainty (whether about the present or the future) but progressively sharper insights."[2]

Gaining Integrated Strategic Insight with Transformational Leadership

An emerging form of strategic insight attainment takes its guide from transformational leadership principles and expresses these principles not in leading others but in the strategic initiatives of the front end of companies. The foundation of this approach is the following framework of how we should think about strategy in times of transformation when there is not much to hang your ideas on.

Principle #1: Transformational Strategy Need Not Be Big and Bold

Strategic insight has always been known to be larger than life. Many of us look for the big idea, the grand vision. We expect new ideas to take our breath away.

But if the principles of leadership are to be engaged in strategy formulation, the quiet must overcome the noise. Hence, we must return to the Gandhian principle that transformation comes only when we realize that we must be the change we want to see in others (i.e., to change the world, let us change our neighborhood, and to change our neighborhood let us change ourselves).

To this foundation, strategy formulators believe that:

- One idea can change all ideas.
- One person can change all people.
- One company can change communities.
- One community can change the world.
- One idea in one person can change the world.

It may seem an exaggeration, but the people of Tunisia turned to nonviolent protests because of two people with principles—one who set himself on fire in protest of his poverty,[3] and another who taught the world about nonviolent noncooperation (Mahatma Gandhi).

So, the concepts that the ideas of transformation and the force of business transformation must always come from the top and that if you do not get the upper management buy-in, then you will not succeed, fall to the past and not the future. When market transformation occurs, the world becomes flat and big companies no longer beat small organizations, because size is neither an advantage nor disadvantage. The leadership of an organization, in a transforming market, and customer beliefs cannot be assumed to be from a top-down framework. History is littered with many a king or pharaoh who believed that top-down is the way to go until one among the masses took charge of a vision for others.

As I type this book, Egypt is experiencing a revolt by its citizens. I am sure that when I begin my edits, history will have written the second chapter to this story. But today, I know that one can change many and that one idea can power all people in transformation. Egypt faced complete transformation as a country when citizens demanded better and then used the internet and social networking to give scale to their efforts. It took 30 years of dominance but less than three weeks to destroy a regime using the voice of one person with one idea that resonated with many who were willing to put their lives on the line. This is a good example of transformation led with leadership principles rather than the classic strategic elements used in business. It was powered from within rather than from the top down.

Principle #2: Strategy Is Not Only an Outward Relationship with Customers and Stakeholders

Classical leaders work to influence others. This may seem a form of market manipulation. Authenticity can now even be manufactured in marketing programs rather than truly realized in marketing programs. But customers of this and next generations live in a highly connected set of communities where communications drive at quantum speeds. They know when they see untruths and manipulations. Organizations' strategies also mirror this obsolete model of coercion: the belief that if we tell the customers what is important they will follow. Herb Kelleher, of Southwest Airlines, stated, "Customers are like a force of nature—you can't fool them and you ignore them at your own peril."

Authentic leaders make the choice easily to speak in their true voice and to the truth as they see it. Transformational leaders market the truth on the front line. What if corporations found this same insight? Strategic business transformation in corporations is more an inward relationship rather than outward marketing push.

Perhaps the philosopher Tarthang Tulku personified corporate insight with the following statement:

> Once we go through a true process of self-discovery, no one can take away our self-confidence; the inspiration comes from within, and we know without needing to be told.[4]

Organizations that think of their strategy as they view how a person can transform others find that the models of transformation of the past are ineffective for long-term transformation. Like Gandhi changed the world by starting with himself, so can a corporation.

Mother Teresa focused on her children and her cause. She believed that everything began and ended with compassion. Her strategy was to be the change she wished to see. She branded her delivery of care uniquely, positioning her message and aligning this message to her real voice. This strategy shined powerfully across the world.

Keshavan Nair, who documented Mahatma Gandhi's leadership style, states that "service to any group—shareholders, customers and employees, or society should be done in the context of service to all."[5] Transformational leadership embodied in strategy can only function when strategy embraces service to all and does not discriminate. It does not worry about competition as much as it is aware of them.

Principle #3: Strategy Is Not about Changing Others' Behavior

Under a similar light, many executives try to affect others' behavior (i.e., buy my product or service). In marketing, we want to change others to think or behave in a certain way. But in attempting to change others we are changing ourselves forever. The truth found in the value proposed to customers must resonate with employees and be deployed with humility to transform rather than pushing corporate audacities to fuel growth. Furthermore, traditional strategy is constantly looking for the ingredients to proprietary advantage that force many to look for the new and differentiated. Transformational leadership teaches us to look for the new ingredients but not to forgo time-tested ingredients of service to others.

Have you ever wondered why one company with the same technology as another wins over the other? We usually explain it away with "they must have been first to market" or "they found the customers who care more and kept them loyal." Frankly, the core to purchases in a transformed market is fueled by a set of key attributes (discussed in the following chapters), but it must be established now that transforming a company can be done by brute force or by a much more powerful and lasting approach that triggers the inner purpose housed in every employee who came to the company to serve a goal. Every employee holds a goal to serve. They also hold a goal to attain wealth among other things to keep themselves alive. But if you can tap the essence of service to others and the reasons they join an organization and connect this to a goal of great importance to society and their future, they will inhabit the cause of the organization and make it theirs. How else can we explain how the Japanese workers who are trying to solve the nuclear disaster in 2011 are working with the knowledge that they will probably perish because of their actions? They are known to have stated that they do it to save others.

Principle #4: Strategic Insight Can Be Taught

Skills can be taught and learned but destiny must be realized. Transformation as a business is based on an insight that the leaders or others find as the driver of transformation. If not, why transform? Strategic insight is about peeling the onion, uncovering the depth that lives within an organization. Organizations are organisms of thought, ideas, and beliefs. We are all humans, but in this humanity we are collectively capable of bringing our knowledge to what we believe is our corporate destiny to serve. Strategic realization comes to the prepared mind. A corporation swimming in the noise of an industry tends to be unprepared. An introspective, meditative, and contemplative corporation gets prepared for insight to visit it. Strategy, for Southwest Airlines, could have been fly airplanes with a point-to-point architecture versus hub-and-spoke architecture. But strategic insight with Southwest Airlines was built on the foundational concept of service—that is, "giving people who'd otherwise not be able to travel the opportunity to do so."[6] Insight like this cannot be taught, but it can be exposed and enabled if the corporation is prepared to accept its destiny to serve.

Principle #5: Strategy Needs Leaders and Not Followers

We often hear of strategic failure being blamed on the lack of execution rather than the lack of insight. "Following" a tactical path is a model of the past. Strategy is about leading to strategy, not following a strategy. But followers within corporations cannot lead in strategy. Hence, the notion of followership in strategy may be ineffective. We may not be able to afford this in the future. Strategic leadership has always been the domain of the elite in organizations. Strategy should be latent in all corporate citizens, customers, prospects, and partners. Great strategies cannot create followers; they create great transformational leaders. This model discards the notion of followership and embraces enlightened self-leaders who partner from common cause. They serve the concept and one another to achieve the goal, which is really anchored on values and truth.

Principle #6: Keep Direction, Not Score

The Titanic measured its way into the iceberg. But this is not the first instance of corporate disasters where measurement took over for direction. The challenges of travel to far-off lands over the water brought about the greatest of all obstacles. Many a ship sank because its crew lacked the understanding of where they were with respect to land. By A.D. 150, however, Ptolemy had reduced the known world into 27 maps and created the first world atlas, which greatly aided ships in navigation.[7] He knew of latitude because the equator was right in the middle of the earth, and zero degrees longitude was the true challenge.

Longitude had to be measured using time—that's both time at land and current time. It took John Hanson, working between 1730 and 1770, to look beyond the stars (the tools of Galileo and Isaac Newton) and find the mechanical timepiece that could withstand the hazards of travel. Just as great ships must chart their position before undergoing ocean voyages, businesses must measure their position and direction rather than measure where they are with respect to false targets in turbulent times. The challenge has been in finding the tools to measure theses organizations' voyage. Measurement is not an end but a means to an end. Measurement is the "measure" of direction—a means to a new beginning. Unfortunately, organizations try to measure everything that they can rather than find direction through their measures or measure the direction taken.

Measuring today's direction is a lot simpler than putting together a strategic scorecard of not just the financial measures but also the directional nonfinancial metrics. Later chapters will build this scorecard. Organizations in transformation must measure both the score and the direction they are taking. In other words, they must feed the mouths of today and find the mouths of tomorrow. Keeping score without direction is inadequate, but keeping direction without score will get you nowhere as well.

Principle #7: It's Not about You; Find Something Bigger Than Yourself

I love my mother. She has never stopped caring or supporting me. I speak to her weekly, and during one of these sessions, I found myself documenting to her how the world was out to get me and that there seems a master plan to destroy all happiness I have enjoyed. I spoke of my work challenges, my friend challenges, my own needs, and so on. She listened quietly and responded by saying, "You know, son, it's not about you. It's about what you do." This struck me strongly. I have now incorporated it into strategy thinking because narcissism is the cornerstone of strategy in corporations. The business plans seems to gush "me, me, me," and we cannot get past ourselves to understand that the real reason we exist is for the service of others who pay us for our existence. The way out for corporations is to find a goal or pursuit that is greater than its own self-consciousness. Corporations with purpose can forget themselves in their pursuits and direct their corporate energies to that single transformational goal. Michael Porter agrees:

> The concept of shared value can be defined as policies and operating practices that enhance the competitiveness of a company while simultaneously advancing the economic and social conditions of the communities in which it operates.[8]

Principle # 8: Can I Get a Witness?

Here is another one from my mother. I was talking to her about how I did not feel appreciated for all the things I do for my family, my work, and my friends. It made me upset that people were taking me for granted and that I was also being judged for not doing enough when I know better. She declared, "There is a witness, you know?" I know her to be very spiritual, and I decided that she was tirelessly reminding me to remember the "person in the sky." But no, she informed me that I was my own witness and that if I do not even respect my own perspective and truth about me, why should I want anyone else to notice me? Corporate strategy is sometimes also this way. Many times strategy is about showing before knowing. Furthermore, you may be the only one that sees that transformation is coming in your industry and all your cohorts in the industry could call you overreactive. Truth as you see it as an organization may force you to commit before you actually can see what that means. Paul Nunes and Tim Breene, in their article "Reinvent Your Business before It's Too Late," confirm:

> Making a commitment to reinvention before that need is glaringly obvious doesn't come naturally. Things often look rosiest just before a company heads into decline.[9]

The eighth principle of transformation reminds us that it does not matter who hears it or acknowledges it: Truth is unchanged, and that is what matters if you witness this. This strategic principle frees us from endless "how do I look good" attempts in strategic sessions and focuses us on a "let's get to the truth" approach to strategic decision making. Too often, we want to do what other people notice rather than get it done for the sake of all.

Linking Strategic Insight with Servant Leadership

In 2002, I wrote an article titled "The Ten Deadly Sins of CEOs" in an attempt to document the experiences of several CEOs I had coached as well as my experience running startup and emerging businesses.[10] I received the most cards and e-mails with regard to one "sin" more than any other: "working without a cause."

Many CEOs believe that their passion is the cause of the company. This is a delusion. Organizations are made up of individuals who have multiple agendas and motivations. Especially in these hard times, individuals are not satisfied with work for work sake and are asking, sometimes privately, what work is all about? To win, CEOs must uncover the hidden common purpose usually found under the skin of the organization.

When I meet with executives, I often ask them whom they admire as entrepreneurs. The answers are as expected—Howard Schultz of Starbucks, Bill Gates of Microsoft, or Les Schwab of Les Schwab tires, to mention a few. When I follow with the question, "Who is your most admired leader?" they often skip any of the traditional entrepreneurs and move to higher ground, mentioning individuals like Mohandas Gandhi, Winston Churchill, or Martin Luther King Jr.

Why is it that many of us hold leaders we admire to a different yardstick than we hold entrepreneurs? Why do we not admire entrepreneurs as leaders? Why do we not consider these great leaders, like Gandhi, as entrepreneurs? After all, the Mahatma managed to motivate forces to perform beyond their self-expectation; he raised funds to meet his objectives; and he hired a startup management team and paid them nothing to free India from domination. He also branded his offering—nonviolent noncooperation. Gandhi dealt with the economics of politics and drove his competition out of his country. His cause had economic consequences. We seem to admire him more as a leader than an entrepreneur maybe because we believe entrepreneurs are profit focused.

I believe that the lesson learned from these great social leader-entrepreneurs is that each had a cause greater than them. Southwest Airlines has a cause to provide the "highest quality customer service delivered with a sense of warmth, friendliness, individual pride and Company Spirit." But let's not also forget that Southwest can make flying fun and inexpensive, too. Organizations that find their cause and reflect it through their optimized business activities win financially over others who just chase profits with their mission statements hanging on walls.

Causes have economic as well as symbolic value. Without an economic focus, causes die very quickly as unfunded feel-good initiatives. Your organization is running on a cause today, but it may not be economically directed. When cause and economics come together, they form the foundation for the linkage between strategy and servant leadership.

Can servant leadership principles serve strategic insight? Greenleaf believed that the "work exists for the person as much as the person exists for the work."[11] One model for work to exist for the person is when strategic insight and servant leaders are aligned to a cause. When we think of work, we also think of being done with work so that we can go live. But the principles of work when connected with us as people, we know that our work is worthy of service to others and can transform them and ourselves. Then work exists for us and we exist for the work.

If corporations can find ways to communicate a strategy of transformation, inclusion, liberating customers, partners, and employees, then strategy will move from bounded documents on desks of planners to the front lines, where true servant leadership can engage.

Servant leadership has always asked us to listen more and speak less. Strategic insight is seldom about analysis and more about understanding needs of customers.

As Keshavan Nair said:

> Every step we take—no matter how small—to understand the needs of the people we strive to serve will increase our bond with them and move us in the direction of a higher standard of leadership.[12]

Summary and Observations

If nations can transform from the actions that start with one person with one idea, then why can't corporations when transformation is anticipated? The principles that guide the transformation of India from British rule and Egypt from dictatorship can also guide the transformation of any organization. This is possible because of the moment in time of our economy; the state of evolution of our corporations; our new social technologies, which are far more immediate; and the state and perspectives of our people.

Armed with these principles of transformation, organizations and the people within them can start to see the unseen with a view beyond themselves and toward the transformation of customers and prospects in need. These organizations can strive for a cause greater than themselves not just as a wish but also as part of an operational strategy. Finding meaning at work powers the twenty-first-century employee population. This population also knows insincerity from truth. CEOs who find truth in themselves will not need to worry about being misinterpreted, but those who cannot feel the plights of customers and people in our society will have to worry because the fuel that drives our new economy fills the containers that bring purpose to profits.

Notes

1   Frances Hesselbein and Paul M. Cohen, *Leader to Leader* (San Francisco: Jossey-Bass: 1999), p. 45.
2   Robert K. Greenleaf, *On Becoming a Servant Leader* (San Francisco: Jossey-Bass, 1996), p. 321.
3   "The Tunisian fruit seller who kickstarted Arab uprising." CNN.com. www.cnn.com/2011/WORLD/meast/03/22/tunisia.bouazizi.arab .unrest/index.html?iref=allsearch
4   Tarthang Tulku, *Gesture of Balance: A Guide to Self-Healing and Meditation* (CA: Dharma Press 1977), p. 84.
5   Keshavan Nair, *A Higher Standard of Leadership: Lessons from the Life of Gandhi* (San Francisco: Berrett-Koehler, 1997), p. 86.
6   Hesselbein and Cohen, *Leader to Leader,* p. 47.
7   David Sobel, *Longitude* (New York: Penguin Books, 1995).
8   Michael E. Porter and Mark R. Kramer "Creating Shared Value," *Harvard Business Review,* January/February 2011, pp. 63–77.

9   Paul Nunes and Tim Breene, "Reinvent Your Business before It's Too Late," *Harvard Business Review,* January/February 2011, p. 83.

10 Mohan Nair, "The Ten Deadly Sins of CEOs," *Journal of Accounting and Finance,* (Hoboken, NJ: Wiley, 2002), pp. 45–51.

11 Greenleaf, *On Becoming a Servant Leader,* p. 321.

12 Nair, *A Higher Standard of Leadership,* p. 73.

Sin #2: Driving without a Cause

Before organizations lose market share, they usually lose their identity. They forget who they are and what they stand for or against. That triggers the lack of coordination of purposeful work toward their customers. Strategic business transformation is based on the premise that a driving force greater than the organizational mission powers the transformation of markets and customers. This commitment to a transformed customer experience and value overshadows all other measures of success. This premise is that once an organization identifies its true calling and energizes the individuals in the organization to act, the organization and its people will identify the necessary skills, plans, and capability to achieve this cause. Rather, most organizations organize their talents and technology and look for the motivating power of making capital without a cause. More often, businesses believe that they must acquire capabilities to win in markets that change and they forget that they must uncover the motivation to energize the core assets in the company—its people and its customers—to really turn the afterburners on. A cause, an organizational purpose for its customers and prospects, is the fuel that engages the mind and machinery of the organization.

Robert E. Quinn, author of *Deep Change: Discovering the Leader Within*, emphasizes:

> I am often reminded of Gandhi, early in his career, in South Africa. He had developed a vision and was working toward it. One day, a man arrived from another country and volunteered to join Gandhi. The man asked, "Aren't you surprised that I've

shown up like this?" "No," Gandhi replied. He pointed out that when one discovers what is right and begins, the necessary people and resources tend to turn up.[1]

Organizations think the reverse is true—that we will organize for success with market analysis, people, and capability analysis and leave the core purpose to the end. For transformation, cause is the ultimate organizer, since there is so much disorienting noise in the market. There is usually enough data to justify any premise because all the variables used in the past to understand your market still exist and seem as if they also will exist tomorrow. The only problem is that the variables that guided your premise yesterday will not guide you tomorrow. They are not the main drivers of transformation because the markets of the future will be driven with different variables.

We tend to believe that we are powered by skills, plans, execution paths, and competitive spirit. Organizations, like people, may attain all the skills, capabilities, but the connecting tissue that holds these attributes together is a purpose larger than themselves—a cause. And when a cause is identified and committed to, the way to the cause can be formed with tremendous vigor and focus. Of course, organizations must build competency and build assets preparing for purpose, but having skills without purpose will not prepare you for transformation. Transformation comes from this source. Transformation, unanchored in a basic belief, becomes incremental change in disguise because it does not have the lift necessary to power past significant and unpredictable disruption. Just as competencies and capabilities came to Gandhi when he was cause focused, a business cause will power the organization to gain what they need to gain to make things happen. Using Mahatma Gandhi as an example may seem incongruent with organizational transformation. Incremental change has its tools well defined. But transformative change mirrors the transformation of great individuals like Gandhi in several ways. The following chapters will bring out these characteristics of transformation.

Transformation Needs Momentum, Not Movement

We will discover market momentum in Chapter 5, and it helps explain the differences between trends and momentum. The rational approaches work well, but other more direct approaches also find truth in our experience. Inspired people perform beyond even their own expectations. So do inspired organizations, which are communities of people who come together for a common goal. Powered by a strong belief, organizations can create a movement rather than just motion. Their belief powers directed action to achieve a set of goals that transform markets.

Death of Mission, Birth of Cause

Mission statements can be uninspiring. They are usually difficult to connect to the work really being done in organizations. The term "mission," based on Latin roots, is associated with tasks assigned. People send you on a mission. Cause is a reason to act or a calling. In this sense, a cause is taken, not given.

Many CEOs believe that their passion is the cause of the company. This is a delusion. Organizations are made up of individuals who have multiple agendas and motivations. Especially in these challenging times, individuals are not satisfied with work for work's sake and are asking, sometimes privately, what is work all about? To win in strategy and execution, CEOs must uncover the hidden common purpose usually found under the skin of the organization. "Human beings just don't put their hearts into something they don't believe in," states James M. Kouzes and Barry Z. Posner in *Encouraging the Heart*.[2] Conversely, mission statements are sad replacements for the common purpose found under the skin of most organizations. They are seldom understood or even followed in organizations because they do not fit the qualities of a cause. The following sections describe the differences between a cause and a mission.

Missions Are Short-Term Actions, and a Cause Is an Everlasting Theme

Missions are part of strategy while a cause leads strategy. It defines strategy focus. Nikos Mourkogiannis, author of *Purpose: The Starting Point of Great Companies*, declares:

> When a company is driven by a Purpose, the vision, mission and values flow naturally from that Purpose. People don't need to be "aligned"—they already have been attracted to the organization, as employees or customers, by its Purpose.[3]

I see much truth in his comments because, more and more, I am meeting young men and women who are not willing to work without life balance. They comment that they are willing to do work but not willing to give up what they believe for work. Ironically, they do not believe in their work and hence want to find other things to do outside of work. So, if an organization can find meaning with them that is also their work, they will bring their passion to work.

Walt Disney rested his entire organization on making people happy, not on making cartoons. He defined this everlasting theme to decide the pathway of his creation, which has lived beyond his lifetime. Sam Walton defined Walmart to give ordinary people the chance to buy the same things as rich people. This too defined a position in the market that is purposeful and has driven Walmart to its greatness.

Mihaly Csikszentmihalyi, in his groundbreaking book *Flow*, explains the psychology of optimal experience:

> In the lives of many people it is possible to find a unifying purpose that justifies the things they do day in, day out—a goal that like a magnetic field attracts their psychic energy, a goal upon which all lesser goals depend.[4]

A Cause Has Personal Implications, While a Mission Has Organizational Implications

Before we go too far in destroying the concept of missions, Peter Drucker in *Managing for the Future* declares:

> Starting with the mission and its requirement may be the first lesson business can learn from successful non-profits. It focused the organization into action.[5]

Identify the missing link in mission statements. They are seldom personal. They are really oriented organizationally. Some missions are really purpose statements and display personal beliefs. But most are void of goals greater than themselves. They are internal and somewhat centric to the world we live in daily rather than driving to a greater more abundant objective. Howard Schultz emphasized "great brands always stand for something bigger than themselves."[6]

Sin #2: Driving without a Cause 51

"Be-cause": Great Brands Find Their Cause, Not Mission

A cause is discovered while a mission is instituted. Take, for example, John Mackey, cofounder and co-CEO of Whole Foods, who said, "I think business enterprises are like any other communities. They can aspire to the highest values that have inspired humans throughout time."[7] He continues:

> I think Whole Foods' highest purpose is a heroic one: to try to change and improve our world. That is what animates me personally. That is what animates the company.[8]

James Kouzes and Barry Posner, authors of *Encouraging the Heart,* claimed:

> We all know organizations—perhaps even our own—that send a team of executives off on a retreat to create a corporate values statement. They return with credo in hand, print it on posters, laminate it on wallet cards, make videotapes about it, publish it in the annual report, hold training classes to orient people to it, and chisel it in stone in the headquarters lobby. Then, they wait for commitment to soar. It doesn't. And it won't.[9]

This is the push method of getting engagement and alignment of the organization to a purpose or cause. Employees do not allow themselves to be pushed into believing in the purpose of the organization. However, organizations tend to blame the process rather than investigate the true elements of getting individuals in an organization aligned. With the advent of the Internet, the social network, the power of communications, and the sophistication of the younger generation entering the marketplace, authenticity is becoming far more of the driver of whether a leader can get engagement. The authenticity of the message, the readiness of the organization to receive the message, and the patience of the customers to see the message unfold slowly are all key ingredients to transferring a core purpose into an organization. One interesting thing about a cause is that it encourages everyone to put their best out for the company. Hence, the model for transformation that is unfolding in this book encourages all employees to bring their authentic leadership into a transformation. Causes are found within the organization, and it waits to be awakened inside one leader among us—not necessarily the upper management. Missions are seldom hidden; they are imposed. Causes are discovered.

People seldom join a company because of the mission but they always join a company because of their cause. They want to "because." A cause brings out the will of the organization; while a mission imposes a will onto an organization. CEOs can find a competitive weapon in identifying and calibrating each individual to the cause. Today, corporations compete in terms of products and services. A few compete in terms of the personality of the cause they pursue. Causes do not have to be all-encompassing. They could be simple and industry specific. But they rest upon an idea for transforming that which is current to a new state that is better for all of your target customers, not just the employees or shareholders. Causes are all encompassing and cannot separate one person from another, and yet causes do divide people based on their beliefs. Causes will not make everyone happy but will force you to choose to join or to fight. Causes live on an edge—the edge of your worldview and your beliefs. We all want to find causes to support, and what brings us to work cannot be just work itself but the purpose behind the work. If you can tap into the cause in them rather than the work in them, you will see a fast-paced sprint in your organization.

CEOs know when they are imposing their will onto an organization and when they are bringing out the cause of the organization. Gandhi brought out the will of an entire nation by clearly articulating his core purpose of using nonviolent noncooperation to free his nation from subordination. Martin Luther King Jr. displayed similar focus on a cause and articulated a method and a dream that drove millions to action.

Southwest Airlines has a declared mission to provide the "highest quality customer service delivered with a sense of warmth, friendliness, individual pride and company spirit."[10] But if I were to attempt to find their cause, it would be that they want to give those who could not fly a chance to do so.

Southwest seems to have a deeper purpose than stated on its Web page, and that is that the airline is dedicated to helping people who have never had the opportunity to enjoy flight and that in a sense they are targeting a grandmother who wants to visit her grandchildren. Organizations that find their causes and reflect it through their optimized business activities win financially over others who just chase profits with their mission statements hanging on wall posters. Causes must also have economic as well as symbolic value. Without economic focus, causes die very quickly as unfunded feel-good initiatives. Your organization is running on a cause today, but it may not be economically directed. When causes and economics come together, they form a foundation for the linkage between strategy and purpose.

Causes Change Us before They Change Others

All the great transformational leaders first transformed themselves before transforming the organizations and world they served. Let us consider Moses, Gandhi, Mother Teresa, and Nelson Mandela and then consider Steve Jobs, Sam Walton, and Bill Gates. They all changed to form the purpose of their organizations. But they found an idea, a vision, and a purpose before their organizations formed or transformed. It may seem inappropriate to consider Moses or Gautama Buddha in the same category or scale as Bill Gates, but for each one of us, inspiration has the same quality of personal impact. One is a massive change in society, and the other may be considered a microburst of product and service business transformation. Yet, history will show how these contributions impact the world at large. They are both personal transformations that melded into organizational transformation. As Quinn puts it:

> . . . the process happens only when someone cares enough to exercise the courage to uncover the issues no one dares to recognize or confront. It means someone must be enormously secure and courageous. Culture change starts with personal change. We become the change agents by first altering our own maps. Ultimately, the process returns us to the "power of one" and the requirement of aligning and empowering oneself before successfully changing the organization.[11]

Hence, organizational change starts with culture change and culture change starts with personal change.

Where Do Causes Come From?

Organizational folklore tends to attribute cause to the CEO or executive staff. That may generally be the case but they are sometimes the ones who articulate the voice of the organization. History has shown us that transformation is seldom kind to the incumbent leaders and that inspiration is usually found in the unexpected, the underserved, or the undiscovered. Therefore, enlightened CEOs and executives engage everyone in the discovery of a cause. Quinn clarifies: "The popular theory is that for a successful change to occur, it must come from the top down, from the outside in." Many organizations think that senior leaders know better and must guide the organization. "However, I also accept a seemingly opposing theory that postulates that an organization and world can be changed from the bottom-up. One person can make a difference."

Best Buy found its purpose through a former CEO, Brad Anderson. He formed his principles from his life as a store manager. He was elevated to lead Best Buy years later and also became vice chair. During his tenure, he listened to his store managers and his blue-shirted teammates. He believes that transformation comes from them and less from the middle managers, who tend to be forced by function of their focus to perpetuate the current business model. Best Buy rose to leadership through his active philosophy and his attitude about driving a core purpose into and out from his people. So in any organization, there is one among you who can lead a transformation in the market.

Can an Organization Transform Markets without a Cause?

An organization without a cause can transform markets. But it is hard work to do so. Financial goals can motivate companies. It is interesting that when we speak of strategy, we use words like "conquer" and "capture." We speak of competition as "destroyed" and "killed," and when we speak of leadership we use terms like "serve" and "guide." This just does not work in transformative markets. People see the imbalance between what we expect inside and what we do outside, and they want it to be consistent. Causes settle that. We must be the purpose we serve, and we must act to improve the lives of our customers and not destroy anything. If competitors exercise their right to be different, then we can destroy that belief for our customers. A cause is a purpose greater than us, and we get lost in our cause rather than be identified as it. Organizations can fail if they become their cause and if CEOs and other leaders think that the cause is about them. When the egos of the organization become stronger than the organization's humility toward the cause, organizations decline in their momentum. Sometimes, they can continue if they are a monopoly in the market and customers do not have a choice. But markets shift after a while. No leader lasts forever, because there will always be one among us who will find a cause to free the others from any business or personal tyranny.

Chapter 10 provides examples of causes and a framework for viewing the organization as a set of attributes targeted from the cause.

Summary and Observations

Missions are different from causes. All too often, corporations run past the reasons for their existence and get to the vision of their future. Employees also run away with the idea of wealth creation, for some time, until they look around for the real reason to come to work and see that selfish goals can only carry them so far. Causes attract and retain the right transformational leaders because:

- A mission is given, while a cause is taken.
- A mission is a short-term action, while a cause is an everlasting theme that guides you.
- A cause has personal implications, while a mission has organizational implications.
- A cause is discovered, while a mission is instituted.
- A cause brings out the will of an organization, while a mission imposes a will onto the organization.
- An effective cause has economic potency, while a mission is unclear in its economics.

I receive the most discussion about causes from CEOs and executives in corporations. Many start justifying their purpose as philanthropic endeavors, and they speak of how much time and leadership they and their leadership team put to others. I think these social causes are wonderful, and I believe in them, too. But we discuss a similar passion when we talk about cause in organizations. In this context, corporations that know why they exist and how they exist to transform willing customers for the better can weather the transformational storms ahead. Without this guiding purpose, people leave when times get tough. Furthermore, they do not stay if they feel that the corporate purpose is inauthentic or not experienced daily and not modeled daily by the leaders in the organization.

Notes

1   Robert E. Quinn, *Deep Change: Discovering the Leader Within* (San Francisco: Jossey-Bass, 1996).
2   James M. Kouzes and Barry Z. Posner, *Encouraging the Heart: A Leader's Guide to Rewarding and Recognizing Others* (San Francisco: Jossey-Bass, 2003), p. 49.
3   Nikos Mourkogiannis, *Purpose: The Starting Point of Great Companies* (New York: Palgrave Macmillan, 2006), p. 54.
4   Mihaly Csikszentmihalyi, *Flow: The Psychology of Optimal Experience* (New York: Harper & Row 1990), p. 216.
5   Peter Drucker, *Managing for the Future* (New York: Penguin Books, 1993), p. 205.
6   Howard Schultz, *Pour Your Heart into It: How Starbucks Built a Company One Cup at a Time* (New York: Hyperion, 1999), p. 260.
7   Justin Fox, "What Is It That Only I Can Do?" *Harvard Business Review* interview with John Mackey, January–February 2011, p. 120.
8   Ibid, p. 120.
9   Kouzes and Posner, *Encouraging the Heart*, p. 52.
10 Southwest Airlines about page. www.southwest.com/html/about-southwest/index.html?int=GFOOTER-ABOUT-MISSION.
11 Quinn, *Deep Change*, p. 103.

5

Sin #3: Missing Market Momentum

Sir Isaac Newton, famed inventor and scientist (note that several great scientists identified momentum before Newton), identified the three laws of motion as he formally explained how objects move:

1. Every object in a state of uniform motion tends to remain in that state of motion unless an external force is applied to it.
2. The relationship between an object's mass m, its acceleration a, and the applied force F is $F = ma$. Acceleration and force are vectors . . . ; in this law the direction of the force vector is the same as the direction of the acceleration vector.
3. For every action there is an equal and opposite reaction.[1]

A very powerful physical example of such force is the 2011 earthquake and tsunami in Japan. The earthquake generated enough force to destroy or damage major parts of Japan.

Essentially, momentum can also be applied to markets. Physical analogies break down quickly, but the essence of strategic momentum of markets, businesses, and buyers explains why customers keep buying coffee from the same place every day or why people will purchase a club membership in January and not attend sessions even though they did the same thing the year before. Momentum is part of everyday activities and continues to build upon time unless compelled to do otherwise. Notice that when a football game goes awry for one side, the troubled team calls a timeout. One reason is for the losing team to gather themselves, and the other is to break the momentum of the winning team.

Why Is Momentum in Markets Important?

In anticipating transformation before it happens, we have nothing to watch or people to ask about what form it will take. All the regression analysis in the world will not predict the answers because as mentioned before, we are basing our regression on an assumption that what happened in prior years will repeat in some form and within a range. Tell that to Egypt. Or in the Middle East when citizens were uprising in peace to declare that they need a new form of governing while telling the world using social media to communicate immediately to the world. Tell that to Circuit City and Kodak in regard to their business models. When a market shifts 80 percent structurally and makes obsolete the 20 percent that was once the original market, we must look at the momentum drivers rather than the trends in front of us. Looking back at the past for answers can be educational but not sound. The momentum drivers that force these structural shifts are key indicators of "true north" as a compass point for us to build our competencies and market programs. People needing good coffee was a trend, while people needing community in coffee was a momentum driver.

If we understand or identify and study the momentum for a transformative future, we can pick up what drives this momentum and decide to stop it, encourage it, or follow it. Anyway, we can use this key understanding to build services and products that serve the momentum and the customers it creates. These momentum drivers will rise above trends in the market and can be captured with great products with purpose.

Measuring Momentum of Markets and Companies

Markets gain mass and have speed in increasing sizes, but that measure is a lagging indicator since it must grow before being measured. Similarly, the rate of growth of a company's market share or profit or revenue (depending on the metric used) in relation to its size could be a measure of momentum as well.

Is momentum a lagging indicator or a leading indicator of market identification? Well, that depends. Momentum is a measure of the pace of the business in growing market as a function of its size and speed of market share attainment. If we are to attempt to identify markets before they exist and watch the momentum of the feeders to this market creation, it would be leading indicators. If we are to watch a growing and triggered market, watch the customers or prospects that are already forming, it would seem a lagging indicator of market identification. The appeal of placing momentum before any other marker for strategic business transformation is that it is the root of all motion if we can identify the key drivers to such momentum and the nature of the customers it is creating. When markets are transforming, maybe four years from now, we can watch the behaviors, trends, and tendencies of the customers and prospects and pick what is driving them in a certain direction and then find a market that is forming. By watching these momentum drivers, we can find momentum and feed it in a transformational market.

What Is Strategic Business Momentum?

Markets form and die all the time, just as markets grow and shrink over time. Markets form with forces that enable them. If we can either identify or enable these forces, we can have a head start on markets that could form. Momentum occurs at the tactical level (e.g., when sales go up because of price or value). Momentum defines itself differently as the movement of a set of prospects with identified desires and is compelled to purchase a solution to a problem they face and want to solve. Momentum is not trend analysis. Regression analysis and trending can get us something, but when we are studying how markets form it is best to look at the drivers that create markets, not at the markets themselves. We may be asking customers if they would like to have ATMs and they, as history has told us, will say no because they like people to talk to them. But when the momentum driver of independence takes over, ATMs become a market served by a product. If we define the market as customer-service-oriented, then we would have lost the hidden message that customer service does not mean that it has to be delivered by a human being.

An example that illustrates the difference between trend and momentum is the stock or financial market's behavior. Since many lost money, the sentiment of many could be to not take any risks or to stay out. We can say that the trend is down, but if we study the momentum driver, we might find that one driver of momentum is be greed or the belief of many of us that we will time the market entry and exit.

Momentum as End Outcome

Organizations invest money, time, and resources to produce products and services to create momentum. They believe that if lucky, the customers who purchase these products keep coming and markets will be created especially for their inventions. Geoffrey Moore, author of *Crossing the Chasm*,[2] defines how technology companies have taken this as gospel as they push products into the market, first with early adopters and then the mainstream. Product managers all aspire to create product momentum this way by analyzing trends, understanding customers, and filling an unmet need in a differentiated way. The underlying philosophy is that products create buyers that create markets that gain momentum.

Momentum as Leading Indicator of Markets, Customers, and Value

Momentum can be found everywhere in dynamic markets. For example, why are people going to college these days? What drives them? Is it a desire to learn? The ease of gaining college loans? The lack of jobs? The momentum driver that is above all this noise is that people want to look better in their own eyes. They want to realize their potential and want to be in the company of others who are changing their own lives. If we tap into this driver and the others discussed, we can create markets by defining the customer, finding the value while discovering a cause to serve in their need. Momentum is created where there is consistent, continuous, and definable movement of prospects and customers who need and want to purchase products or services as solutions to an inherent desire or need. Think of momentum not as surf coming to shore but as the currents that drive all wave motion. In steady-state markets, businesses create products to serve the needs of their customers or prospects. Businesses asked them, and customers tell the business what they want. Then the new products create customers, who then form markets in motion, and if they grow fast and the business succeeds, the company and the market gain momentum.

In markets that are changing and transforming, customers are also forming, and they cannot tell you accurately what is up and down. So watching the momentum drivers of the markets (i.e., the subtle movements based on high-order needs that people always respond to) can give you an understanding of where the momentum is going. For example, when Howard Schultz moved on Starbucks, the coffee sales in the United States were trending down:

> A market study would have indicated it was a bad time to go into the coffee business. After reaching a peak of 3.1 cups a day in 1961, coffee consumption in America had begun a gradual decline, which lasted till the late 1980s.[3]

Yet, he believed that he could bring a new form of coffee and community to the market. He saw the need for community and a third place. He brought that momentum driver into focus and created a market, which attracted customers and then satisfied a product demand. We all know that couches, coffee, and conversation existed before Starbucks, but they did not exist in the way Mr. Schultz envisioned it as a driver of a deep need for community. In transformative markets, one must find the drivers and serve them with excellent differentiated product or service.

Momentum Drivers

Since we are watching for momentum in markets that have not yet formed, watching for things that drive momentum might be better. Momentum is the result of some force. Here are some examples of drivers:

Trends	Momentum Drivers	Outcome
Disk storage	How about storing it somewhere safe	Cloud technology
Coffee	Community in coffee	Starbucks experience
Tires	Trusted tires, local communities	Les Schwab
Minicomputers to PCs	Engineers needing more control	Personal PCs
Electronics	People need help at home	Best Buy

Difference between Trend and Momentum

Trends are movements in the markets where we can identify a direction of purchase, and these tend to be linear progressions of the market behavior. For example, the aging workforce is a trend. But the momentum driver in this context could be that no one enjoys aging gracefully or living beyond their savings. A trend is that people who age want to look better as they age. A momentum driver would be immortality as expressed in plastic surgery or the urge to bring back the past in music and other entertainment. Trends show that more people who are aging purchase fancy cruises, hair color, and cosmetic surgery. But if the market is transforming with new inputs like Medicare being challenged, more people dying of diabetes, the children of the baby boomers being unemployed because the older players are not leaving due to the financial crisis, the momentum driver for most of this would be preservation of dollars and dignity.

Mistaking Movement for Momentum

Momentum is a function of market velocity and mass. It is the combined value of mass (size of market) and velocity (the speed of change or adoption). Movement is only one axis of momentum and, frankly, something to put on the organizational watch list.

Most business planning cycles are three to five years. Hence, speed or velocity is viewed in that time frame. Exhibit 5.1 isolates a way to view the components of momentum, namely velocity and mass. It is a simplistic diagram identifying the nature of the organiza-

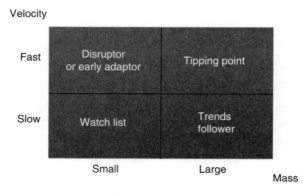

Exhibit 5.1   Relationship between Organizational Velocity and Mass

tion that engages in any or all of the four quadrants in its philosophy. Certain parts of an organization can display the tendencies of velocity and mass relationship. It is a gross generalization to place an organization into a box of this nature, but it is meant as a guide not a measurement. In addition, parts of an organization may work in any of these quadrants. However, if the net momentum of an organization falls in the lower left quadrant, the organization must review its performance and get better.

Momentum drivers can be either emotional or rational. They defy the need-versus-want categorization mentioned by Adrian J. Slywotzky, author of *Value Migration*. He frames needs and wants in context of a far more multidimensional approach to understanding opportunity. He states:

> Need refers to benefits and feature of products that customers would like to buy. Most market research focuses needs. But what customers really want is the result of a complex decision-making system.[4]

What momentum driver drove iPad sales? Was it the intuitive user interface? The unique collection of applications? Apple was not the first to introduce the tablet PC, but it brought new life to the industry as a whole with the iPad. The iPad invigorated the industry because it had horizontal appeal and usage in multiple industries feeding the momentum driver of personally intimate and portable productivity and entertainment. The iPhone created momentum for personal productivity as well. Momentum like this creates markets; markets create customers; customers purchase products. Or possibly the momentum driver was that people yearned to be part of a club that supports design over functionality and inexpensiveness.

The iPad entered the market the same way Apple entered the smart phone business, with elegance and usability and an integrated platform. The value benefits that drove purchases and a new market is expressed best in the way a customer reflects on it: "The iPhone are considerate to me." The personalization power and the unique features bring the high-order value proposition of being considerate to the user. Apple did not invent mp3 players, nor did it invent the smart phone or e-books. However, in all these products that served needs, namely the need for music download, the need for phones that are personal organizers, and the need for a 30-second instant book, Apple found the unique momentum drivers that it served with the iPod, iPhone, and iPad. Apple used all its assets and unique brand to create markets from momentum drivers found beyond trends and products. Apple reinvented the category with an eye to what momentum it creates in reinventing the way people interact with computers. It seems looking back that many mp3 players, e-books, and phones viewed themselves as technical products serving a need not a momentum driver of usability and creativity. They also viewed themselves as products when Apple built platforms. A product is a unit of value that someone purchases and that is sold to them. A platform is a unique set of tools and services combined together to attract many products or applications into its portfolio. The iPhone or smartphones have many applications but also are phones. Hence, they are a product as well as a platform of for other applications.

W. Chan Kim and Renee Mauborgne use the term *trend across time* to describe momentum:

> Three principles are critical to assessing trends across time to form the bases of a blue ocean strategy, these trends must be decisive to your business, they must be irreversible, and they must have a clear trajectory.[5]

They continue:

> . . . with the technology out there for anyone to digitally download music free instead of paying $19 for an average CD, the trend toward digital music was clear. This trend was underscored by the fast-growing demand for mp3 players that played mobile digital music, such as Apple's hit iPod. Apple capitalized on this decisive trend with a clear trajectory by launching iTunes online music store in 2003.[6]

But Apple is usually credited with producing products that people never knew they needed until they experienced them. So it seems that it subscribes to the "build product, create customer, create market, and then gain momentum in the market" approach. But an alternative view of its strategy could also be appreciated here. Consider that Apple could have tapped into a momentum driver with the mp3 player market as it introduced the iPod. There was already a trend for mp3 players, but downloadable music was not at its center. iTunes brought that into focus after Napster tried and failed in its business model. The combined power of iTunes and iPod formed a momentum serving a new market of music enthusiasts who wanted an elegant way to personalize their relationship with their music. These same individuals were forming the basis for personal productivity platforms taken by the iPhone and the iPad.

Mentor Graphics Corporation, a leader in design automation software, grew significantly in the 1980s in delivering the connected solutions for design engineers. The obvious need for connected and concurrent engineering processes drove the market trend but what drove the purchase of workstations with software was the momentum driver of control that engineers needed on their own desktop and that engineers needed to feel in control of their designs. This driver has never changed and only grows stronger. The rationalized and communicated benefit is better quality and performance of the engineering team, which buyers will tell you are the reasons for purchase. The emotional value of workstations at that time was that engineers could work in a concurrent environment and hence produce a higher-quality product. But the emotional momentum driver was that their engineers needed the best equipment and also a sense of control over their design. Workstations gave them both. The market trend was identified as the movement of minicomputers to desktop workstations. Did workstations drive the market momentum, or did the need for engineers to own their own workstation for the comfort of control bring the acceleration of the market? It is natural to consider that products create customers and customers create markets, and markets then gain momentum. This would be viewing momentum as a lagging indicator of market performance.

Exhibit 5.2A illustrates the momentum impacts. In transforming markets, products are not pushed onto customers, who readily buy

We believed that products find customers, who create markets. Then markets in motion create momentum.

Products

Customers

Markets

Momentum

Exhibit 5.2A   The Market View of the Past

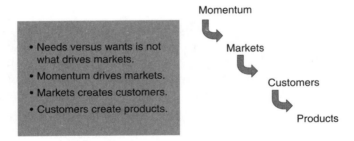

Exhibit 5.2B   Momentum Drives Markets

because they believe that today will be tomorrow. Customers are confused and cannot understand the future. In that case of a transforming market, they tend to wait unless you find a driver in them that believes emotionally and purchases rationally. In these times of transformation, we must find the momentum that will create markets, that create customers who purchase products (see Exhibit 5.2B). Transformational times demand that we find the momentum hidden deep inside customers who can trust their "true north" as guide. We cannot find this in the rational without the emotional. Also important, that the drivers we find in prospects can be manipulated by organizations or we can take the higher road and find true value to improve the customers in whatever they want to achieve.

Momentum Is about Customers in Motion

Momentum is about finding a powerful and lasting desire that has not been met and that transcends the basic features of trends and fads. It is a desire that connects the target customer to the cause of your company. It is a desire that seems everlasting and that can withstand the current market chaos. For example, when we think of why people buy products, we usually say that they are attached to the brand or that they identify with or see themselves in the product. Momentum is beyond that argument of need and want. It is about subtle but powerful movement of the target customers in transforming themselves. Great transformative companies tap this desire and feed it for the greater good. The Internet was first a vehicle of war, designed to protect our world from the loss of communication in case of an atomic attack. It has morphed in its value proposition because ultimately the momentum it served was a desire by all to connect and not necessarily to be failsafe. It has become the vehicle of transformation in communication. The ultimate driver for this could be the need to connect and the need to be validated by others.

What in the world has happened to us? We stand in line to pay for coffee that 10 years ago we could not pronounce; we bark words in code that only you and the barista can understand; we do not even use the word "large" to describe the size of a cup; and we spend $5 or more for a good cup. We watch 300 channels of television, sometimes on an iPad, and pay for movies that we download. We purchase cars that have no resemblance to the vehicles we grew up with because they have hard drives, mouse controls, and traffic and navigations systems, along with back seats that massage you while you watch you 300 channels of television. And yet we are nostalgic about our old movies and old shapes, like the Mustang we used to drive. These conflicting desires live inside us.

If customers are staying rational in their purchases, why are they purchasing a flat-panel screen television, which is almost the size of their first apartment? Rational buyers do exist somewhere, and they rationalize emotional purchases. Yet they are customers who did not exist a few years ago. They created themselves, and a market was born. Business purchases seem to be more rational, but as the saying goes, "you never get fired for buying IBM," which implies that any business purchase has emotional and political overtones of safety and trust. In transformation, customers are born and markets are created. Momentum creates customers. How do we define and understand them?

New Customers in Old Clothing

It does not mean that a whole new set of customers are born, and it may imply that underneath your prior customers lies the new client. We know that if no one buys, you don't have a sale. Also, if no one buys consistently and regularly, you don't have a business model. In transformational times, momentum drivers create the momentum of a set of customers who consider options in a different way than they used to. For example, buyers of phones shifted from basic to smart over a period of time, and now many only want to have a phone that does more. The most telling experience occurred recently when I was watching a sunset. A person nearby stated, "I wish I had my phone" when he was thinking of taking a photograph of the sunset. These customers would have rejected the idea of a phone and camera combined in the past. This is transformation at its best. When customers don't even know that they have changed, how do you find out what they want?

Oh Where, Oh Where Are Your Customers Now?

Customers can leave at any time if they find value and price somewhere else. The brand of your products and services and your company can keep them, but customers migrate as the markets transform because of a new momentum driver. We see this in the concept of cloud-based technologies. Translating to the person on the street, it means that she may no longer need a disk to back up her files because she can store all of her important things on the Internet and download them anytime or synchronize them anytime. This momentum of safety and convenience is coming along fine, and its impact will be seen a few years from now. Notice that many computers are becoming smaller and thinner because they are void of large disk sizes and drives. If you were in the storage device business, what momentum driver would you be looking at to understand the customers? Even among the most loyal customers, there is one who is fighting to make a change; if you do not provide it promptly, transformation will leave without you because there are many disruptive influences that will migrate them. Customers who used to back up their computers weekly now move their data to a cloud-based backup service and entrust their life information to these teams. What was important before (privacy) now is second to convenience.

In transformative markets or in a business that is to transform, we must keep an eye on our existing and new customers, if they are not the same. Corporations, which understand what they are, what they prefer, and how they purchase, find their way through transformation.

Tactical and Strategic Customer Segmentation

There are two levels of understanding customers:

1. *Tactical.* Who are the customers? What do they consider value? What are their behaviors? How do they purchase offerings? Who are their influencers?

2. *Strategic.* What do customers believe in? What are their decision criteria? What system of prioritizing value do they deploy? Are there emotional and symbolic triggers that attract or reject these customers? How do we define the space customers live (segments)? Are there micro segments of behavior or personality, ethnicity, affiliations, worldviews, purchase capacity? Who do these customers influence?

All these facets influence our view of the customer. It is inadequate to define customers just as segments divided by age or gender as in the past. In transformation, businesses that refine their view of the customer along several axes and aspects will find them and satisfy them. The basis for any strategy is the customer target. If you believe that you don't have a target and that you provide a horizontal service or product that everyone will use, either you are going to be very successful or you have made a big mistake in your assessment. Both ways, if you are working in a transforming market, you must identify your core customers and then expand unless you have unlimited resources where you can have multiple parallel teams work.

Finding the Key Target Customers

If you were to ask the people in your organization who your customer is, what would they say? Would they be consistent? What if you were to ask your colleagues why you have these customers? Then continue with questions like "are they going to be our customers seven years from now and why?" What do you expect your answers to be? What assumptions are they making in their responses, and are they valid? The first anchor of research for transformational markets is understanding where the momentum drivers are taking us; then focus on momentum as through the eyes of the customers.

The second anchor of any market research is identifying the customers and the premise of their behavior. Yet that seems to not be done often, because this is not an easy thing to identify. In a complex business and market environment, customers may seem broad and narrowing the target too much only excludes the others. Take a toy store, for example. It may be safe to say that the customers are children of any kind. Another analysis may bring about that parents are the customers. A third analysis would declare that grandparents purchase many of the toys in our country. Then, what about relatives or friends who attend birthday parties? Then, there are a number who don't buy toys because they cannot afford it. We segment these customers to find the right ones who can afford toys and live close to the stores. Do they drive? Are they working? How do they respond to the mail we sent them? Do they watch television? Do they avoid the commercials? What is their mindset about certain toys? These questions help you formulate a premise about the customers and slowly draw a silhouette of your ideal customer so that the business can test all aspects of the delivery of value against this frame. You may also develop personas of these customers and identify an ideal personality and worldview for each of these "target" customers. Then consider that in a complex purchasing environment you may be selling to several types of customers in the same business. One may be very economically oriented, thinking about the financial impact of buying your product; another may be focused on the usability and the application of your service or product; another might be very concerned about the implementation and support of your product or service; and, finally, someone might be focused on helping others make a decision. He or she is probably an advisor, an educator.

John Donovan, Richard Tully, and Brent Wortman, authors of *The Value Enterprise*, state:

> . . . managing for enterprise value is a big departure for many managers and, indeed, business theorists. They believe that catering to one or two constituents will automatically guarantee the others will be taken care of. This is a grave mistake.[7]

So, in a larger business, these four actors play roles in the decision to purchase our product or to engage your service. The four actors are usually one who considers the economic questions, another considering the points of view of the users, then one who is coaching the deciders, and then one who considers all the practical implementation issues. You should consider all these factors but not lose the focus on who is the main target customer.

Behind Every Customer, There Is Someone Else

For every purchaser, there lives an influencer to the purchase or someone who really controls the purchase. I call this person the "fox" in the purchase decision. The fox really decides for the decider. For example, CEOs decide on a financial decision, but most of the time the CFO weighs in heavily. In health insurance and health-based decisions, the subscriber makes the purchase, but in many cases the spouse of the subscriber makes the decision. The purchaser represents other purchasers in the decision, and they are the foxes in this purchase. Once you uncover this, you can consider how you satisfy that purchaser as well.

This would require that you have a multidimensional view of your customer and his or her relationships to the truth as they see it. Linear definitions of a customer will not apply in a complex transformational environment. Organizations must know by interviewing prospects exactly who to accept and reject as their customers. If everyone looks like a prospect, then you have no prospects.

If you build your definition of your customer like you build a cube, where each side is a new variant, then you are building a picture of your customer in multiple dimensions. The center of the cube will represent the collection of all the coordinates of this customer.

Observe Behavior and Inhabit the Customer

Many organizations send out teams to interview and survey customers. Some perform focus groups, while others observe customers in their natural habitat so that they do not lose aspects of how their customer lives. This has proven very successful as a way to uncover things that even the customer is not aware of.

Honda sends its engineers to observe customers in their natural environment to understand how they can design, build, and solve human problems and challenges. The U.S. Honda design team spent time in Disneyland in a parking lot when they were considering trucks for their customers.[8] Honda sent a design team to Europe for a whole year to do nothing but observe the relationship between drivers and their vehicles.

One of my key marketing professionals brought me two workups of advertisements so that I could choose which one would go on a billboard. I asked him what our customers thought, and he lamented that the focus groups were scheduled but not ready. I asked him to go the restaurant across the street and ask any random stranger to give advice and keep doing it until he knew. He was shocked but followed my request. He returned with much data and, moreover,

wisdom of the relationship between the advertisement and the customers. These are all appropriate methods for uncovering and
understanding the customer you want to serve. But to move from
identifying the customer to identifying with the customer to truly
designing for the customer, you must inhabit the customer's identity.
Inhabit means understand the emotions, the ideologies, perspectives, and decision-making criteria behind all of the customers'
activities. Inhabitation is about living their way for a while, and it
involves being them rather than watching them. Transformation
impacts customers in unpredictable ways, and you must see through
their eyes and feel through their hearts to find the answers and the
direction of their motion and momentum. Formal methods lead you
only so far, and the rest of the journey is up to you. You must care
enough to allow the customers to take you over.

Summary and Observations

Let us recap the differences among momentum drivers, momentum, and trends:

- *Momentum driver*—forces that influence momentum
- *Momentum*—the movement of prospects of mass; the desire to
  purchase product/service with velocity
- *Trend*—general direction of purchase or behavior
- In the future markets where the unknown unknowns dominate, momentum can be studied as a leading indicator of
  which markets are forming that can create customers who
  form for a need that we can serve with products. In some
  cases, products create customers that form markets that generate momentum. Here, momentum is viewed as a lagging
  outcome of movement.
- Needs and wants are irrational and rational desires, respec-
  tively. Momentum drivers can be any force that instigates
  lasting momentum.

According to *The American Heritage Dictionary of the English
Language*,[9] *trend* means: "A direction of movement; a course; a flow";
and *momentum* means "product of a body's mass and velocity."

Momentum is a unique way to view the market. Many times we
think of markets as static, at least when we take a look at a company

or business. They are constantly in motion, shrinking and growing. Since markets are dynamic, it would seem obvious to consider them moving with mass—momentum. Even though the physical laws of motion are not applicable, they are an appropriate framework in which to view these markets in motion. We see momentum every day in our lives and also in our thinking and views of the world. It is important to see them as a market attribute that is a very powerful tool for good.

Notes

1   Newton's Three Laws of Motion. http://csep10.phys.utk.edu/astr161/lect/history/newton3laws.html.
2   Geoffrey A. Moore, *Crossing the Chasm* (New York: Harper Collins, 2002).
3   Howard Schultz, *Pour Your Heart into It: How Starbucks Built a Company One Cup at a Time* (New York: Hyperion, 1999), p. 32.
4   Adrian J. Slywotzky, *Value Migration: How to Think Several Moves Ahead of the Competition* (New York: Harvard Business Press, 1995), p. 13.
5   W. Chan Kim and Renee Mauborgne, *Blue Ocean Strategy: How to Create Uncontested Market Space and Make Competition Irrelevant* (Boston: Harvard Business Press, 2005), p. 76.
6   Ibid, p. 77.
7   John Donovan, Richard Tully, and Brent Wortman, *The Value Enterprise: Strategies for Building a Value-based Organization* (New York: McGraw-Hill, 1998), pp. 18–19.
8   C. K. Prahalad and Gary Hamel, *Competing for the Future* (Boston: Harvard Business Press, 1996), p. 104.
9   William Morris, *The American Heritage Dictionary of the English Language* (Boston: Houghton Mifflin Company, 1976).

Sin #4: Ignoring the Two Orders of Value

During the economic downturn, the public fanned the flames of anger, frustration, and anguish. People stopped buying luxury items; other reconsidered their expenditures, moving in lockstep to products and services that were lower in cost and perhaps value. Are these temporary market-driven changes, or are these signs of a transformed market? Michael Treacy and Fred Wiersema, authors of *The Discipline of Market Leaders*, offer:

> Customers don't pay price premiums unless they perceive that product to be worth the extra cost, which means that product leaders can't set outrageous prices. To customers, brands are nothing more than the product leaders' implied promise—the promise to deliver unmatched value. If prices exceed the value of the promise, the product leaders' edge disappears.[1]

In a transforming market, driven by momentum, customers can change in their view of value and migrate to products that provide more value for the price or to less expensive products with just enough value. The skill comes after you have identified the momentum of your customers and prospects; you now want to match your value to that momentum and give them what you believe they desire. In new markets, however, you may not know what they want and they may not be able to articulate what they want. While you focus on the momentum drivers that guide their purchases and participation, we must also consider what value of your product or service compels buyers to purchase your product instead of others'. Your value should align with your cause and align with the momentum in the market you have chosen.

Adrian Slywotzky adds to the true challenge of understanding value:

> Value migrates from outmoded business designs to new ones that are better able to satisfy customers' most important priorities. A business design is the totality of how a company selects its customers, defines and differentiates its offerings, defines the task it will perform itself and those it will outsource, configures its resources, goes to market, creates utility for customers and captures profit.[2]

Many times we think of one level of value—the rational and the emotional. These two components of value seem to cover all the aspects of why someone will look and purchase your product. The rational value proposition is explained as all the technical, practical, and logical reasons why someone bought your product; the emotional is the feeling one has in anticipation of and after purchase.

Car purchasers reconsidered the value of high-end vehicles for two reasons:

1. The cost of the car was challenging.
2. They did not want to look rich even if they could afford it.

Interestingly, the people who crawled their way to wealth to show it now want to hide it. Even though the buyers of luxury vehicles gain value in their purchases, they now are considering the symbolic value of the message they are sending others. This is a new form of value beyond the rational and emotional aspects. A higher-order value proposition is that you are accepted or admired by your peers for making sensible decisions in purchasing a "sensibly priced" vehicle.

As markets transform, the momentum of certain segments of a market can drive customers to think differently about what they believe value to be. Transformational organizations reorder value in the new markets they want to address and try to find the sweet spot to capture the attention of the customers who are migrating. The two orders of value are:

1. *Low-order value propositions (emotional and rational).* This is value derived from the benefits of the service or product you are viewing. It is rational. You compare the benefits that products provide. Second is the emotional dimension. These are your feelings about and attachment to a project.
2. *High-order value proposition (symbolic).* You symbolically attach to the product or the company that sells the product. You identify with the purpose of the product and what it stands for. It is symbolic for you to participate and with your purchase you are declaring to you and your peers your intention to be a different person in the world.

A hybrid vehicle satisfies buyers at both levels. Namely, the value they derive can be:

- *The rational.* I chose the vehicle because it gives me more gas mileage (low-order value).
- *The emotional.* I feel good that I am doing my part to save energy and it is practical for me to own this car because I save on gas. I look like a participant (low-order value).
- *The symbolic.* I am on my journey to becoming a good human being who cares about the people around me and am sending a message to others that the world needs our attention (high-order value).

What is the power of such value propositions in our markets? The average grocery store will ask you to consider paper or plastic when you are at the checkout line, but Trader Joe's has convinced their members to bring bags that they bought from Trader Joe's to collect their own groceries. The customers of Trader Joe's are participating at both levels in acting to save paper or plastic and to recycle bags every time they visit. This has huge economic value for the company because it saves on costs of bags, but the consumers do not see it that way. Consumers see themselves aligning with the grand vision of a better world without excess, and they believe that Trader Joe's is conforming to their worldview authentically. What force drives customers to believe that they are contributing to the universe when they carry a grocery bag back to Trader Joe's? What makes them permit Trader Joe's to dictate that they will participate in the savings of costs for the cooperative? Is it logical, emotional, or symbolic value that they are deriving?

Low-Order Value

Value derived from products and services is often mistaken for benefits that a product or service provides. Value is made up of three components:

1. *Benefits*—the features and attributes that you like and want to purchase
2. *Price*—the cost of purchasing both in the financial and the nonfinancial
3. *Cost of conversion*—the cost of moving from what you have now to the new product and service

Value is understood to be the residue of the benefits minus the cost spent on purchasing the product or service inclusive of the cost of converting to the product or service. When you buy a new house, the emotional residue of the decision is found in the benefits found in the home, the location, the neighborhood, and so forth minus the cost of the home minus leaving your previous neighborhood. This is the operating definition of a value proposition, and it has limits. If we try to boil life's behavior into one small linear equation, life would be simple and incorrect. When a purchaser views a product, he or she first sees the products' benefits, both functional and emotion. Then the purchaser considers the price and how to move to the product. What is left behind—the emotional, rational, and symbolic value after the subtractions—is the residual value of purchase. This equation helps us understand the drivers of value:[3]

$$Value = benefits - price - cost\ of\ conversion$$

When customers consider a purchase, they look at the benefits of the products (usually the features), the price, and the energy, cost, and time it takes to convert from what they are doing now to what the new product requires. The residual benefit received after this is what the value is to that customer. The high-order (symbolic) value proposition cannot be described with a formula. It represents an aspiration in the customer to identify with something greater and to serve a purpose greater in his or her purchase or participation.

It is not just about the customer making a statement, as in the emotional value proposition, but about the customer making a declaration about a life purpose and it is sometimes about telling themselves rather than the world around them. For example, some people become vegetarians for health reasons (rational), for not killing animals (emotional), and for a declaration that all creatures are created equal and that it would be nonviolent to declare their connection to the world (symbolic). It is about the greater purpose of how we choose our identity and how we identify with others in our community. It is an expression far beyond gaining emotional value from a purchase. It symbolizes meaning in purchase and it involves a stand you take.

Momentum of these customers toward their aspirations can drive the understanding of value to them. An example of this is the iPad. It was aspirational for Apple's iPhone and iPad customers, who wanted the next thing introduced. The momentum of these customers has created a market for ubiquitous personal productivity products. Apple did not invent the category, but Apple assembled technologies into an incredibly usable offering. Furthermore, in transforming markets, value may require new ways of deriving value—inventions and innovations.

In Apple's early days, customers identified symbolically with the company as the company for "the rest of us." It was the upstart that took on the Microsoft giant. This was symbolic not emotional. The users gained emotional value in being part of a club of people who liked elegant design and closed systems.

With Starbucks, Howard Schultz did not just sell a bag of great coffee in the usual channels, namely grocery outlets or 7-Elevens. He refocused the entire value proposition to engage all the senses of his prospects. Schultz may have declared in his book *Pour Your Heart into It*, "Nothing matters in our business than the taste of the coffee,"[4] but he credits his retail operations head, Howard Behar, with the following statement: "We're not in the coffee business serving people, we're in the people business serving coffee."[5] Schultz and his leadership team designed a new way to view great coffee. Starbucks created an experience with coffee and a market for "social" coffee. They created a venue, a third place, the extension of the living room: a place to meet, to gather your own thoughts or be around the conversations of others. Starbucks framed a new language to create this uniqueness, and this was consistent with the customers who gathered.

Again, the two orders of value are playing together to form this recipe of success. Let us attempt to place these in the framework:

- *Low-order (rational):* I like the taste of good coffee.
- *Low-order (emotional):* I like the experience as it is personalized.
- *High-order (symbolic):* I belong to a community, but I am different in my taste. I am in the community, but I am unique because I have unique taste in my own recipe of coffee.

Ironically, most people who go to Starbucks to be part of the community don't seem to want a community to talk to them. They find their common place, keep to themselves, and communicate. It is a gathering place where two conflicting values collide comfortably— one is that I want to be part of a whole and the other is I want my privacy. Try to sit with someone and talk to them, and you may not be welcome. Starbucks created a cultural transformation and a coffee transformation. People speak of Starbucks less in terms of its coffee and more in terms of the reinvention of the customer experience.

Facebook serves two levels of value to its customers. There are many segments of customers who are on the networking site. Consider the younger audiences and their value:

1. Low-order value would be to connect with friends in a simple way (rational). The low-order emotional would be to have friends and have others see that.
2. The high-order is the need to belong, to have your own pack but also to reach back into your life and enrich your existence with memories that continue in real time. For the older generations, it seems the high-order is to find old friends and to "realize" life once again. The low-order value may be similar to the younger population's. Aging populations have similar needs to realize the value of their lives.

Southwest Airlines's value proposition is stated on its web site: Warmth, friendliness, individual pride, and company spirit for the employees that translates into the low- and mid-order value propositions of low cost, on time, and fun. Southwest's high-order value is subtle but definable. Many other airlines take themselves seriously because of air safety, but Southwest assumes that you are worried about safety and makes it fun for you to fly again. It started with the "love airline" as its theme and moved to the "fun airline" today. It also symbolizes freedoms with its commentaries and advertising statement that "you are free to move about the country."

Symbolic Value Propositions

Value must be aligned with what the corporation believes in, or else the corporation will not attract the targeted customer with the ultimate goal of transforming the customer experience and then the customer view. Alignment of the market's momentum, the target customer, and the high-order and low-order values of the organization is essential in surviving and thriving in transforming markets. It is in this business and market design that success is found.

How Do Momentum and High-Order Symbolic Value Differ?

High-order value is about the way that you configure your product and service to uniquely identify with the momentum drivers that last a long time in your customers' minds. If they are driven by things greater than themselves, like doing their part to save the planet, then asking them to purchase a Trader Joe's bag, which symbolizes a club membership in a unique organization with a message, gives the customer a way to participate in service to the greater good. The customer knows full well that Trader Joe's is saving money, but he or she trusts that that money is applied to saving them money on items they purchase while all sharing in the symbolism of conservation. The high order is not a repeat of the momentum driver but a way that the organization exercises that momentum driver and symbolism to lock the customer into a behavior that is enjoyed without manipulation but with agreement.

Truth and Value Propositions

Everywhere you go, someone is trying to convince you that something would be good for you. You often don't even know that you need something until they tell you that you do. So we all go along and watch our televisions, read our devices, and appear to be convinced. But the world is fast changing from this passive role for consumers to an integrated and participative engagement with the Internet, social media, and other forms of action-centered purchasing. The buyers are getting more and more sophisticated, still somewhat blinded by brands, but they are asking for more and are seeking authentic relationships with their sellers. Customers want to trust that the companies they purchase from not only sell good products but that they also stand for the beliefs that customers believe. They want to be led by these beliefs.

The high-order symbolic value propositions are driving the overall purchases of transformed markets because buyers want to hang onto their beliefs and are resisting the urge to give up their basic identities to the organizations. *Satyagraha* is a term coined by the Mahatma Gandhi in his pursuit of freedom for India. It means holding onto truth or "soul-force."[6] This philosophy, combined with his value proposition of *ahimsa*, nonviolence, transformed many of his followers and freed India from British rule. The high-order value propositions that corporations assume as they align the value of their service and products to the momentum that they see in transformation must show this authenticity or they will be sent away by customers seeking truth as value.

The Power of Symbols

Have you had a root beer? I bet you think of quenching your thirst when you see a picture of a root beer. I understand. I don't. I think of something far more emotional and comforting when I see a root beer. Let me tell about a boy named Gage. He is 10 years old. Gage suffered from a rare form of cancer that attacked his spine and he could not grow. He suffered from this challenge for most of his life. I knew and loved Gage. One day I was arranging a bowling party for kids of the Big Brothers Big Sisters organization and decided to invite Gage for the first time just to spend time with him. When he arrived, I asked him, "What would you most like in the world?" I was prepared for anything, because I knew Gage was suffering and he deserved anything he wanted. He said "A large root beer." I remember running up to the counter and demanding the largest root beer they could find, even if they had to leave the bowling alley to do it. They provided the largest root beer they could, and I presented it to Gage whose eyes were as large as the sun. He carried that root beer constantly and enjoyed the gift I gave him. Many days later, I received a gift in return from Gage's father, who brought me a drawing that Gage drew of my experience with Gage and his view of the bowling experience.

A year after that, I met Gage coincidently at a store around the Christmas holidays as he was shopping with his father. I asked him if he remembered me and he said, "Root beer!" When I asked him what he was doing, he reminded me that the season was one of giving and that I should be doing exactly that—giving.

Gage has passed and we are all sad that this little angel has left us, but he reminds us constantly that we all have a higher purpose.

So when I see a root beer, I see more than most. I see a message from an angel. I see a wonderful encounter with a very special person who gave me a universal message of purpose. When I taste a root beer, I relish the taste so much more now. That is the power of symbols in our lives. They represent the undercurrent of value that even a small object can represent. Product and services are nothing without the power of symbols that represent truth as we see it.

Putting Value Together

Value propositions at the high-order are the center of gravity of any transformation. It is here that the value to the customer gets realized. If this is not designed into your products and services, the promise you make your customer is viewed as incomplete and inadequate. The marriage of cause, your core purpose, with an understanding of the momentum drivers that create momentum to target customers who are looking for value at two levels is the way value is derived for transformational companies. Now we can add to the relationships by considering how to power the value proposition with actual competencies that a transformed market may want. Without competencies, how do you deliver the value and in what form?

A cause powers an organization to provide value to its clients. A cause elaborates a greater purpose than a mission and brings about a core ideology an organization commits to pursue. Value is the actual impact to your customer. The high-order value propositions are subtle but can have significant impact.

Summary and Observations

Value proposition is not a new concept to marketers, but it loses some of its core considerations when we speak of the value to customers in a way that convinces them of a false identity in their purchases of products or services. We identify value selling with slimy positioning statements that are completely false and believe that whenever someone speaks of value they mean manipulation. That is so true when it comes to the general idea of value proposition. That is why this topic is so very important. Truth is the ultimate game changer, and the ability to sell truth is a talent not found in many organizations.

We know that value migrates and customers change their view of value. This is about the low-order value propositions. Customers seldom migrate from high-order symbolic value propositions because it is part of what they seek. Wanting to serve others is a value proposition that transcends almost everything, even selfishness. You may think this naïve, but the world is filled with stories of selflessness without regard to reason or logic. The need to connect is a value that is living its destiny in Facebook. This value also expects certain trusted authentic supports to be very evident from the custodians. For example, trust in privacy is the one key element of Facebook that it cannot violate, but if it does, an honest mistake is tolerable. Authenticity becomes the new game changer in value propositions.

Notes

1   Michael Treacy and Fred Wiersema, *The Discipline of Market Leaders: Choose Your Customers, Narrow Your Focus, Dominate Your Market* (Reading: Addison-Wesley, 1997).
2   Adrian J. Slywotzky, *Value Migration: How to Think Several Moves Ahead of the Competition* (Boston: Harvard Business Press, 1996).
3   I want to thank Dr. Lynn Phillips (www.reinventures.com) for introducing me to the formula v = benefits—cost in a seminar he taught at University of California Berkeley many decades ago. I modified this formula to include the cost of conversion. I also added two levels to value: high order and low order. I stress that the rational and emotional value proposition is very valuable and placed in the low order view not be misinterpreted as less important. In fact, both the high and low order value propositions should be considered. The high order is the unseen symbolic value that has surfaced in transformative markets that I address as well.
4   Howard Schultz, *Pour Your Heart into It: How Starbucks Built a Company One Cup at a Time* (New York: Hyperion 1999), p. 249.
5   Schultz, *Pour Your Heart into It*, p. 250.
6   Eknath Easwaran, *Gandhi the Man: The Story of His Transformation* (Petaluma, CA: Nilgiri Press, 1972), p. 41.

CHAPTER 7

Sin #5: Overlooking Transformational Servant Leadership

The new organization is a workspace with no walls. Leadership styles of the past cannot conform to the unbounded workspace commanded by remote employees, portable tablets, portable computers, and worldwide internetworks.

Hierarchical management techniques and paradigms are breaking down. Matrix management is trying to bend the iron bars of the hierarchical organization to make it "look" better rather than "be" better. These management paradigms were built in an era that assumed that the employee was a mindless participant in the management's adventures. Today, we can walk into the hallways of certain global Fortune 500 companies and it would be like finding a lost civilization that still believes archaic customs like management memos, large group meetings, and, even more historic, interviews for jobs. This managerial hypocrisy has led employees to breed a responding hypocritical loyalty. They will promise to not look for the next job on company time! And yet everyone is asking for leadership and direction—the two drivers of business today. They want someone else to direct them and someone else to lead them. The answers to a transformed environment, however, do not lie outside these individuals but within them. They have yet to look within themselves for the very things they need for them to be leaders. In a sense, the more we look outside to bring our insides into the work transformation, the less we see it because everyone else is doing the same. When you add to this equation the variability and confidence of jobs, we end up with a very quiet and docile management environment that fears change and forces change by this very fear.

With sweeping transformation in markets and customers, organizations first must decide whether they are the broom or the dust. Brooms bring about change, while dust responds to change. Brooms gain speed with force, while dust waits to be moved but adapts. There is not room for a broom that does not clean or for dust that believes it doesn't need to adapt.

Many business leaders have built their organizations under the principles of command and control. In transformation, these organizations can move fast only if the leader is right the first time and can see all and know all. The function of the effectiveness of transformation of such a company depends on the capability of the leader because in this control environment, what the leader decides is what is done, with very little input because fear is the substance of engagement. Transformation to an empowered and adaptive organization is different because the employees participate in the design and decisions within the company and so the entire organization works toward a goal to bring transformation or to adapt to it.

Even if we wanted to, leaders cannot control others. They can control some of the conditions that others work in. In attempting to control others in the organization, we fall prey to false assumptions. For example, we assume that people must be managed, when they must lead. We assume that people are a problem to be solved rather than the ultimate corporate asset. The challenges the twenty-first century brings us cannot be dealt with using seventeenth-century thinking. In a transformation, in this new world of leaders, there is no need for the role followers take (i.e., just tell me and I will do it). Rather, they want other leaders in their own right to lead when they need to and follow when they need to. Hence, followership is not a job but a role we take given the circumstance. With no trace of followership, leaders drive you to hire other leaders, not followers.

What does it mean to rethink the definition of management? Employees, having found freedoms, are left to their own devices with little to no understanding of the rules of this new engagement. What then become the new rules of the leader? We hear of the dictator changing to coach and the teams turning to self-managed groups. Can the previous definitions of leadership apply?

Organizations focused on transformation of the present should be populated by project-centered self-leaders who partner with one another when needed. This can take minutes or years. It all depends on the mental maturity of the team you assemble. The team that is populated with self-leaders knows their limits and knows when to take risks. They are self-driving yet compassionate. This team seldom plays "we-they" with the formal leader. I am often asked, "What does a transformed leader organization look like?" I reply, "It looks just like any other except it behaves very differently." Our human skeletal structure is very similar, but our bodies and minds form unique footprints in our world. So why do we mistake the skeletal structure with the way the nervous system works in organizations? Similarly, organizational architecture, although important in traditional organizations of leaders and followers, cannot control the movement of the collective minds of its inhabitants in a leader-transformed organization. As mentioned before, we understand that rank and organization exist, but the organization chart is like the skeleton of the body—it holds things together but is hardly the way the body works. In the transformed organization, the CEO rests his anxieties and leads him or herself. He or she must understand that he is not the only driving force; his people have their own.

The transformation from the current hierarchical managerial order to this transformed leader organization will demand the abandonment of the current approaches of single-minded command and control and the adoption of dramatic inner change, self-reengineering, and self-identification with corporate goals. In other words, it is about personal change creating group change that triggers corporate change, and not the other way around. This does not mean that we wait for the leader to arrive, as India waited for Mahatma Gandhi. It does mean that the smart CEOs will know that they do not drive transformation; they are catalysts to it. The yet-known leader within or outside waiting to enter will lead this transformation. There are times when the CEO is the leader chosen by the people, but he or she must earn that right not by rank but by his or her own personal transformative power, which comes from tremendous introspection, self-testing, and realization. This is what this chapter about leadership is about.

But this change can be dangerous if the organization is not ready. Before anything, we ask the fundamental question "whom do we lead?" Under the transformed-leadership paradigm, all of organizational concerns can be solved if approached from the self outward. We all lead ourselves every day. We partner with one another with common goals and aligned inner visions. Some organizations are populated with followers who demand to be led. These organizations cannot be directed to self-leading methodologies instantaneously. They must evolve. The current managerial "fad" is devoted to empowerment, but if it comes too soon (i.e., from darkness to light) employees will run blind at the harsh transformation. In some ways, companies doing this find that their productivity drops quickly as their employees, who lack guidance, stare like a deer at the headlights of an oncoming truck. Self-transformed leadership starts from introspective leaders. Without self-discovery and introspection, leaders are playing a role in a defined space. As the management and business space trends more to the undefined than the defined, the role-playing leaders are failing in their traditional leadership. New leaders are emerging to fill these gaps that markets in transformation create.

Increasing Our Choices of Transformational Leaders

I ask my audiences to name memorable entrepreneurs or business giants that they admire, and they usually name Bill Gates, Steve Jobs, and Howard Schultz, to mention a few. When I ask them to name the people who have transformed their lives, they mention their parents, religious figures, Lincoln, Gandhi, and Martin Luther King Jr., These two questions consistently create similar division between those who they believe are business entrepreneurs and those who transformed their lives, but the audience seldom considers these transformative leaders as business entrepreneurs because they believe entrepreneurs are money makers while those who inspire them emotionally and spiritually are not entrepreneurs. But did not any one of them build an enterprise?

Although the responses are justified, they are misguided concepts. For some reason, we do not connect entrepreneurship and enterprise building with great transformative leaders like Gandhi. But they were entrepreneurs and builders of enterprise as:

- A brand that lives forever—based on an enduring set of ideas.
- A cause that engages the masses into action beyond their usual path.
- Financial models that destroyed the business models of those who oppose their ideology.

- A represented mission, vision, and values that sustained an enterprise of millions of followers who would endure violence and ridicule without payment.
- Their believers pay to sustain the business model of these admired leaders. It is as if employees were paying to sustain the purpose of the business of the enterprise.
- Their teams assembled competencies, partnerships, and funding, and they brought down the opposition.

The perceived difference between great social and religious leaders and business entrepreneurs can be summarized as follows:

Admired Life-Impacting Transformative Leaders

- Driven by purpose beyond themselves.
- Personal brand lasts forever.
- Propelled by a cause.
- Develop followers who model leader.
- Measured by self-sacrifice that leads to national and international transformation.
- Supported by stakeholders who furnish the dollars for the efforts.
- Seeking to create a legacy of transforming behavior and thinking.

Admired Business Leaders

- Driven by self goals.
- Driven by financial gains.
- Developing a brand for the business.
- Dominated by products and service created.
- Rallies small groups and builds enterprises.
- Measured by providing new products and services to transform industries.
- Raising capital.
- Measuring legacy by corporate strength and market share.

These general perceptions about business leaders being self-motivated and social reformers being unselfish is unnecessary and leads us to wrong conclusions. Why do we believe that the people who have transformed our lives and the lives of others are not business entrepreneurs? Why is this important? It is extremely important because the leaders of tomorrow who transform businesses will also transform lives and cultures. Strategic business transformation is based on the premise that transformative leaders follow the principles of the admired, socially effective, virally impactful leaders like Gandhi, but they also build financial enterprises that sustain business models that last. As we tend to believe that admired leaders are in a category of their own for their selflessness, their pursuit of community needs, and their sacrifice, the new leaders for transformational markets have to take lessons from them. If lasting transformation is the purpose, then these traits must be understood.

Business news is filled with business leaders who fight one another and their ethics. We are almost immune to the shocking news of any CEO or executive team who indulges, and we seem to expect it. Business is so underestimated that we tend to believe that ethics equals compliance, although they are different terms. Ethics is a way of being and acting, while compliance is following rules. One is about character and dealing with dilemmas, while the other is about correct actions. The result of indiscretions is the loss of faith in our business society. It is as if our world went to a level lower in its expectations and justified crude capitalism without controls as just the way it has always been.

The Era of the Transformational Leader

Leaders surface when the moment demands them. History is abundant with tales of great leadership moments. Movies, books, and sacred texts display leaders emerging when the need is greatest. It seems that transformation for business into new markets may require this emergence. We call these leaders transformational servant leaders to identify their unique contributions to society not by their personal contributions but from their ability to design organizations that transform society and respond to a transformed market. From Moses to Mahatma, they all displayed very few signals of their capabilities and destiny until something brought them to this realization. In a sense, they were building toward a realization that awakened all their capabilities to lead. None of these leaders took classes in how to transform the world. Very few even wanted to do anything great and in fact seemed to be running away from such things. The lesson for business is that the new form of leader will surface not from the succession plan but from the rank and file or from the outside. The transformational leaders may seem completely out of the system and in many ways radical, untrained, and unsophisticated, but there will be something they say or do that hints of their destiny to transform the organization. Some business leaders have left the confines of one organization because they were never recognized; they intend to build transformative enterprises elsewhere. The enterprise they left may not have understood their potential to lead or respect their contributions for the future. So how does a management team uncover transformational leaders from within? Brad Anderson, former CEO of Best Buy, is a good example of a leader who understood this key element of transformation. His leadership sensitivities are discussed later in this chapter.

The Ultimate Transformational Servant Leader

The leader who self-leads is not concerned with the politics of the office, the lack of respect he/she receives, the productivity of the team, or the revenues. The self-leader first understands his objectives, enjoys the journey, and creates the conditions for self-leading in others. He believes that people are inherently good. They must be given the chance to shake away their follower tendencies and lead themselves. There is no room for negativity, politics, backbiting, or "the dog ate it" excuses. The constant babbling of excuses or reasons is the target of the self-leader. He understands his nature but does not submit to it. He defines this weakness so that he conquers it by putting it in its place in his perspectives. He does not accept mediocrity because it is a cancer. He is compassionate but firm to his targets. He realizes that not everything is black and white but realizes his responsibility to define reality in the way others may need it to be seen. He is caught up by the moment but always creates the conditions for the best performance by his best people. He removes political "cancers" in his organization, so that life continues to grow around him. He is a fierce competitor to his own ego and to others who work from a basis of fear, anger, and manipulation. He understands the legacy of his spiritual inheritance and creates understanding through his day-to-day activities. The ultimate leader creates the self-leading environment in phases, realizing that nothing is created fast. He cleans house by selecting his best potential self-leaders and removes the nonleaders who are unable to adapt to the excellence criteria. He does this only after trying to create the conditions for others to awaken their innermost need to lead themselves without ego and mental prisons. He allows all around him to forge a new leadership mission with the fires of day-to-day trauma. He will tire sometimes but looks to solitude for rejuvenation. Even when others are around him, he can live in solitude. The ultimate leader is seldom understood because he seldom seeks understanding. He seeks only to understand. He never leads, because he seeks to be led by his vision. He seldom teaches, because he seeks to be taught by his experience. Most of all, the ultimate leader is a self-realized individual with an urge and drive to do two things. The first is to create people better than him who can lead transformation; and second, the ultimate leader likes to win the markets of today and tomorrow.

Transformational Leadership: The Ultimate Journey

Have you noticed how many leaders last awhile and then fade away? How many times have you stood by the water cooler in conversation about "whatever happened to so-and-so?"

Transformative leaders display both these capabilities—the art of creating markets and the art of leading others to them. So what is the ingredient that creates these transformational leaders? What is transformational servant leadership? Is it born or is it created? If it is created, what forces create it? Can organizations capture these forces?

The search for these answers is the ultimate journey and one that involves diving deep into informal psychology, ancient philosophies, and the practical experiences of great leaders like Mahatma Gandhi and Winston Churchill. Great organizational leaders are similar. But the ultimate answers come, not from reaching outward to observe their behaviors and successes so often found in books about them, but inward, inside their minds and experiences, where the essence of true transformational leadership was created and lived. Many books and articles have attempted to define and conquer leadership, but many who have read them return with unanswered questions when it comes to how these leaders are created and transform the world view. What causes leaders to become transformational leaders? How do they form a transformational force and challenge the status quo? Can we learn from the experience and realizations of these great leaders and try to uncover the formula that creates leaders who can transform the organization one person at a time?

Leadership beyond Traits

We can only go so far when we teach traits, skills, and techniques. Today, leadership is taught like a science where traits and techniques are studied and emulated. Inspiration is relegated to the "foo-foo" or "soft stuff" that makes most hard-core managers shake their heads.

Comfortably and surgically, we have taken apart the mechanics of leadership, breaking it down into actions and practices. In the 1930s, American society began its courtship with the study of leaders. Now in the twenty-first century, our role models seem to fail us and our leaders don't seem to last because we have mastered the skills that leaders perform but have found it difficult to understand the nature and essence of leadership—the flint that sparks it. We seem to struggle because we all believe that our initial excitement with a certain leader will surely end in disappointment. We have become cynical and unreasonable because we expect perfection with our leaders but allow it in ourselves. We set a standard for leadership that no one can achieve, especially ourselves. It is a Superman syndrome of sorts.

There are many theories as to why leaders don't stand a chance with us. One that I hold dear is founded in how we got here as a nation. We ran from tyranny of leaders in Europe and Asia. We struggled to build a unique democracy that believed in self-leadership and individual achievement. We did not want any monarch telling us what to do. Then in the centuries following, we formed our own monarchies—movie stars, sports figures, TV personalities, and businessmen and businesswomen. But our belief that monarchs must be dethroned has not left us and so we go about bringing them to power and spending the rest of our time destroying them almost as a way to repeat our beliefs in our daily actions.

Max DePree, author of *Leadership is an Art,* put it well when he stated that leadership is serious meddling in other peoples' lives.[1] He understands the fundamental flaw in leadership where we are torn between the moralities of giving all employees their hopes and dreams while ripping their heart out for the sake of the corporation. The ultimate learning a leader gains is one that forces him to live in the world of business but not to be of this world of treachery and deceit and politics.

For many organizations suffering from leaderlessness, leadership takes the form of an autocratic bully or a benevolent fool when it comes to business design and strategy. Leadership becomes a list of mechanical attributes trapped in the body of a human pretending to lead rather than a leader who transforms the world around them. Attributes like "change agent," "hiring the right people," "listening," and "influencing" fill the list. More and more, we are teaching prospective leaders that they are elite while the ones they are to lead are mindless automatons who want and need to be led. We have even convinced people that they are destined to be followers. Describing leadership by someone's attributes is like trying to describe a tree by all the variations of its leaves when the true elements are found in the entire structure, starting with the seed. Organizations try to remember every definition about leadership they can find. I once consulted for an organization that employed a team of executives to document every possible definition of a leader.

To capture the essence of the subject, it seems that they must not remember all these formal definitions and perceptions that trap them. They must learn to forget these imprisoned perceptions about leadership and expand their thinking to embrace other views. Carol Orsborn, author of *Inner Excellence at Work* and founder of Overachievers Anonymous, declares that if "we change our beliefs about the nature of business and of life, we will change how we manage."[2]

What Is Transformational Servant Leadership?

In a nutshell, transformational servant leadership is found in people who:

- Embrace transformational ideas and plans and turn them into business and societal transformations that protect and enable organizations, their employees, their customers, and the general public to embrace, enjoy, and enable financial, societal, personal, and business growth.
- Realize that transformation starts first at the person level and moves to the organizational level rather than a top-down orientation to change.

- Have a sense of service and thus a sense of self. Serve the greater good not just in philanthropy but also with a direct societal impact to their strategies and tactics. They are guided by the greater good and a personal gain but balanced in that priority because it fuels their momentum to creating markets where society can grow.

So, how must we look at transformational leaders to help them survive and then transform our companies? Consider the following changes that we need to make before we can understand the transformational servant leadership.

It Begins Inward

The classical managers' work is to influence others. Great leadership enthusiasts define leadership as a technique to get others to follow the agenda of the leader. This will work for the short term and will also gather gullible followers. Transformational leadership whose goal is to serve customers is about leaders who find their true destiny in the transformation of the current circumstance to something much better for others. It begins with a great deal of self discovery and introspection; walking the walk; and also courage to see the change coming and to force others to see and prepare for it. We can't fake authenticity. Some even have learned to master the art of sincerity. I am still haunted by the memory of one of my direct reports who was emphatic as he declared, "I can be sincere. I've learned how!" Authenticity is a powerful tool of the transformational leader. These leaders can feel that you are desperately trying to believe in what you are trying to convince them about.

Robert Greenleaf, founder of servant leadership in his seminal book *The Servant Leader Within: A Transformative Path*, states, "And if flow in the world is to be remedied, to the servant the process of change starts in here, in the servant, not out there."[3]

Furthermore, transformational leaders are less interested in being noticed for their work. They acknowledge themselves from within. A few years ago, I was engaging in self-indulgent conversation with my mother over the phone. I spent much of the time telling her that I was not being acknowledged for my superb accomplishments. She politely stopped me to remind me with "you do know that there is a witness to everything you do?" Knowing her to be a spiritual person, I acknowledged her reminder that God was watching me and that I should feel good about that. But she corrected my acknowledgment and told me, "No, not God. You are your own witness." This reminds me that if I have the awareness that I am my own witness that I am my own witness that my witness is all I need to what I do, then it comforts and also empowers my actions even further. Transformed leaders witness their own activities and seldom gain acknowledgment and frequently don't care about it.

Management is changing others' behavior to perform what they seldom wish to do; transformational servant leadership is finding what matters for the greater good and others and giving them the tools to win.

Many executives try to affect others' behaviors without realizing their own transformation. In both transactional and transformational theories, we have observed and taught how to change our surroundings to get an intended action. We have seldom realized that we also transform as part of the process. If we also do not change as part of the transformation, how do we remain authentic to the process? People know to trust someone who truly represents the transformation that the leader expects of us. In changing others, we are changed. In convincing others, we make commitments that are contracts with ourselves. In all situations, self-transformation is the key source and catalyst for significant organizational change. Mahatma Gandhi is a guiding example of such a transformation. He self-led and others followed his ideology, not his person. True and lasting leadership is seldom found in the transformed but more in the transformer. Lasting leaders changed in the process of changing others. In fact, they were too busy changing themselves first. Others just saw them transform and joined in. For Gandhi, the great soul, trauma visited him when he was traveling on a train in South Africa. Before this moment, Gandhi was traveling to help his family at the request of his parents, who were getting rather tired of him at home. After all, he was not amounting to much as a barrister and he wanted to be so "English" anyway. Thirteen years after this event, Gandhi spoke eloquently about his philosophy of nonviolence and noncooperation to many who were ready for violence against the British. He had been building his learning throughout his life and the moment arrived. He motivated without attending a "how to influence people" course. He moved the masses with sheer inner awakening. His convictions were built from reading the Bible and the Bhagavad Gita. Gandhi did not display any power over creating a brand in his actions until those moments visited him, and it seems that it hit the right person. One wonders how many people have been traumatized and not responded except in anger or disgust but not through a transformation lens. He spoke to his followers not as followers should be spoken to but asked them to lead their own destiny. Just as a mother would wish of her children to be independent, Gandhi wanted an independent India. When trauma struck, Gandhi seemed ready. Then he created the concepts that began this transformation. Truth and nonviolence were his watchwords.[4] Two words that can melt the world's hearts even today powered him: "nonviolent noncooperation." They have powered many movements since, including the civil rights movement led by the Reverend Martin Luther King Jr. in the United States.

It Must Be Realized and Experienced

Skills can be taught but your leadership destiny must be realized. In the same way, leadership can only be realized. Greenleaf states:

> Leaders are not trained; they evolve. A step-by-step conscious striving will produce something, of course. But a continued synthetic person is not as likely to reach that level of servant leader as will one who has evolved with his or her own natural rhythm.[5]

Nikos Mourkogiannis, author of *Purpose*, agrees:

> Leaders do not simply invent a Purpose; they discover it, while at the same time developing a strategy and ensuing that Purpose and strategy support each other. This requires that they listen to themselves and their colleagues, and are sensitive to the moral ideas, as well as being aware of the commercial opportunities offered by the firm's strengths.[6]

Great leaders know that they cannot create other leaders, but they can create the optimum situations for others to become leaders and lead. Many folk stories tell of well-planned leadership journeys, but very few are true. I believe that people have learned skills to lead and have succeeded using them. We are all only human, but in this humanity we are born with certain powerful inner knowledge of our destiny. This destiny is flexible to transform to any form our mind and spirit dictate.

Transformational leaders do not believe in coincidence; they create coincidence. Transformational leaders learn the art of letting coincidence meet a prepared mind. Leaders prepare for years to discover a new idea when the circumstance presents itself.

Regardless of the circumstances, we find people moving from rags to riches. But we also see the opposite. The easy way out is to say "It all depends on the circumstances . . . the luck of the draw . . . being in the right place at the right time." It does depend. It all depends on you and your mind-set—being in the right place with the prepared mind. Transformational leaders are constantly preparing for an event to transform them. They do not wait for circumstances to change them or give them what they desire; they create coincidence because they take full advantage of a transformative event. Many times, they prepare their own view of the world with its own ethical dimensions. When Gandhi was thrown from the train in South Africa for being in the "wrong" class of carriage, he could not believe that a barrister from Cambridge like him would be told to stay in third class. He did not accept this condition and almost thirteen years later created the coincidences following by pushing forward with burning passports in the front steps of the British government. Then things started moving forward with event after event, which he faced with his ideology and courage, making every moment count. Similarly, Howard Schultz of Starbucks was a coffee buyer when he created the idea of forming a new community of great coffee drinkers when he was in Italy. If I had been him, unprepared in my mind for these coincidences, they would not be a coincidence but just an observation on my part. His was a prepared mind and skill set that met a coincidental concept that spurred an entire industry and a new culture.

Steve Jobs, the icon of genius in the modern world, also believes in coincidence. In a speech at Stanford University, he stated that one couldn't connect the dots going forward but only when looking back. You have to trust, he said, that all the dots will connect in the future. If we believe that we can connect the dots down the road, we will be confident with following our heart's choices today.

It Believes in Transformational Moments—Leadership Events

Moments that bring transformational servant leadership out of people are not all dramatic. Sometimes, leaders discover their true destiny in simple, nonconfrontational ways, but they are still events in which a leader realizes what he or she has to do and be. We could isolate leadership events (i.e., moments when people changed from their normal selves to become leaders). At these moments, certain preconditions fell into place before they transformed. For Mahatma Gandhi, certain undeniable forces collided within him when he was unexpectedly discarded from a train trip across Natal in Africa. He was thrown out of the train for being a person of color who refused to leave a first-class seat. He found himself in a train station in Maritzburg, his luggage and overcoat lost. "It was not his own injury or humiliation that infuriated him; it was the much deeper cancer of man's inhumanity to man. . . . "[7] The view of his world was shattered. He questioned the validity of the British-ruled world. He could not understand why a British-trained lawyer from London could not be allowed to join the first-class portion of the train. But he was Indian. He was not allowed. He asked why a handful of British officers could control a large population of Indians. He asked why he could not be in the same bus as a British citizen when he was a British subject. This explosion, within him, was triggered by trauma, the first precondition for true transformational leadership. It seems that trauma forced introspection for this true leader. They say that if the soil is fertile, the tears of trauma will bring growth! Gandhi is the example of how a shy man can turn to be a strong leader once he finds a force of service to others and a purpose beyond his own ego:

> The man who had been unable to talk in court to enhance his own career would find within himself the resources to speak and write and organize effectively to relieve the distress of others.[8]

Leadership emerges from the collision of five forces: trauma, vision, awareness, plans, and skills. We will isolate and discuss each of them later in this chapter. These forces collide violently and in sequence. It is as if the collision shakes leadership out of individuals who are ready, as if they reconstruct themselves from the shock of realization.

Abraham Zaleznik, Harvard University professor, states:

> Leaders grow through mastering painful conflict during their developmental years, while managers confront few of the experiences that generally cause people to turn inward. Managers perceive life as a steady progression of positive events, resulting in security at home, in school, in the community, and at work. Leaders are "twice-born" individuals who endure major events that lead to a sense of separateness, or perhaps estrangement, from their environments.[9]

Would-be leaders turn inward after a collision of strong and powerful forces. They find themselves challenged when the view of others defies what they believe to be correct.

Gandhi never really mastered the physical skills of leadership prior to being titled the "Mahatma" or "Great Soul." Prior to his leadership event, Gandhi was a soft-spoken barrister who found it challenging to speak in public. He hired a dance instructor and a French teacher and even tried wearing a top hat to become "English." Before he became the Mahatma, he was an average man with average skills and plans:

> As a youngster, however, he lived a double life. At home, he behaved in one manner, with strict adherence to his mother's ways; with his friends, however, he secretly smoked, ate meat, told lies, and wore non-Indian style clothing.[10]

Years after his leadership event, he found his tongue and became the voice that moved 300 million Indians. It was as if shock reorganized the very mental molecules inside him. The skills that we so often identify with him emerged as a side effect of his true transformation. They too looked inward. They too became self-leaders:

> Just to meet him (Gandhi) was to run the risk of being turned into a hero, and the lives of countless numbers of ordinary men, women and even children were transformed completely by this one little man, who demanded—and got—from everyone the highest order of selflessness and love.[11]

So, our model of leadership is not one that is conveniently called "empowerment." Empowerment has its place in the leadership quest, but empowerment comes only after disempowerment. The self-leadership model we are describing is built on first moving inward then reflecting out to an audience that witnesses the actions caused by your inward reflection. They too move inward witnessing the event. This event is what I call the leadership event. This is one of enlightenment rather than classical empowerment. Call it the "ah-ha" or anything else. Every great leader had this happen. They live together only after self-leadership happens.

Transformational servant leadership requires this inward view to ignite to be sustaining. Otherwise, it is only a rehearsal for the real thing.

It Does Not Believe in Followers

Followers are a model of the past. Followers do not exist in the new organization. We cannot afford them. Hierarchical organizations suffer from followers. They follow the person in the hierarchy as well as the objectives of the organization. Followership is about leading to purpose with others who believe the same way. In the obsolete model of the past, they are told what to do and are afforded only the information and control for their job. They are "empowered" by their management, which took power away from them earlier! Empowerment is the new gift from the management monarchy. Organizations and individuals must understand that empowerment is earned and taken; it is not a gift but a responsibility. Real leaders know this right up front and without argument. In fact, they accept it with grace and with a strong understanding of the consequences. A Fortune 100 company designed what it called "self-managed" teams representing product teams to decide and build services that the company sells. These teams resisted many of the suggestions of the management. Empowerment can be granted only to leaders who have attained a strong realization of their purpose. Without grass-roots leaders like this, nothing gets done continually and consistently. You may be able to pump up one event that succeeds but to make it run all the time, real individual leaders are needed.

Leadership, to the traditional organization, is the right of the elite. Leadership, to the new organization, is in all people. Many people don't take leadership roles at work but some lead families; other lead church groups and some lead Scout troops. It is also defined by the leaders in the organization who believe their role is to "take" a leadership role, rather than create leaders. Transformational servant leaders cannot create followers; they create other leaders who serve. He can be called a guru, which in Sanskrit means destroyer (gu) of ignorance (ru). In parallel, leadership must symbolize the "destruction of the idea of followers," or the creation of other leaders.

This new model discards the notion of followership and embraces enlightened self-leaders who partner with one another for common purpose. So, take the concept of followership out of your mind and give everyone the respect they deserve. Transformational servant leaders lead to a concept and a cause that they follow. Hence, they follow as well as lead. Many "followers" will not be able to adjust to this newfound freedom. Followers perpetuate the myth of traditional leadership as well. They are trained to follow the vision of the leader. They believe that they cannot be informed or think globally. They leave reward to the higher powers. They are not responsible until they are recognized as managers or project leaders.

Max DePree, author of *Leadership is an Art*, contends that followers must be granted rights.[12] Only then can leadership function properly. I contend that followers have to realize their true leadership potential first. So does this mean that hierarchy must be destroyed? And what will the new organization look like? The current organization does not exist anyway, so just leave it where it is. Let's form the new leading organization in our minds. If we just discovered the human body, we would realize that the skeletal structure keeps us upright and allows us to function but it is one part of a larger complex but elegant activities that drive us. Transformational servant leaders tend to work with everyone regardless of the hierarchy of the organization. They want to reach out to what makes the organization move forward rather than the formal structures.

Great leaders did not rush through their lives and activate all their intentions. They pondered their ideas. In fact, they paused to assess the situation, challenged ideas first in their mind, and then committed to action. We can assume that the greatest prisons, besides the organizational barriers, they broke out of were their own mental prisons. A leader's journey goes nowhere but inward between the mind and the heart.

Everyone is already a leader and only needs to discover the latent power within each of us. We have been taught to believe that we don't possess the skills. That is secondary when we are considering the spark that creates leaders.

What are we to do? Do we just wait for the preconditions of leadership to confront us? Do we create the artificial conditions that emulate these preconditions? The answers lie in the context in which the questions are asked. Let's change the context and platform of our questions and take a fresh look at this intriguing and beautiful gift of leadership.

Are Transformational Servant Leaders Born or Made?

They are both born and made. The argument in this book is that every one of us can and do lead in many ways. Consider your neighbor who fills his day with nothing but gardening. Is that an act of leadership or is it not? Self-motivation turned into action is leadership, yet we believe that leaders must have followers and without them great change won't happen. This is somewhat true, but leaders start with themselves; without leading themselves, they have no chance to impress others. Furthermore, leadership is a journey, but if we judge the journey and the trekker before they even start we have lost the essence of the learning we must have—that everyone can lead if given enough coaching, focus, and luck. But business' least available resource is time, and given big change demand we may not have the inclination or the time to grow budding leaders for the challenge just in front of us.

This is also understandable, but is also the reason corporations spend so much money hiring from the outside and not developing leaders inside. This also has its problems, but we cannot judge one way to be the only way in transformation—do it your way but realize that transformational servant leaders exist in the quiet of their own minds and not in front of you as leader. You have the power to bring the conditions for them to bring out their true desires for themselves and for others.

There Is One among Us

Transformational servant leaders can exist anywhere in the organization with varying impact to the transformation of the market. If we believe that leadership comes only from the executive suite, then we fail the first test of the market transformation. It will come from all over the organization, but if we believe that the overall leadership of the organization through the transformation is a one-time change, then we fail the second test of transformation, which is that it never ends. Hierarchical leaders in our organization must watch, encourage, and find transformative leaders who are service oriented in the organization daily. These are the ones who will lead tomorrow, and one of them will spark the future vision within them. Believe this and realize that the world does not assume you have a seat in the ship that transports the organization past the challenges of the future. But if you agree with this notion and believe in the purpose of the organization and want to find the leader, you will focus so much on this that the entire ship will be filled with motivated leaders who will ensure that you and the ship will sail past the turmoil and will design its systems to protect and provide for the future.

Transformational Servant Leaders Do Not Display All the Skills to Lead

History has shown us that many of our admired social, political, and business leaders did not come from environments where they practiced all the skills they use to lead their constituents. In fact, some started to exhibit their skills and plans only after some traumatic event brought their entire belief system into focus. Some of these great leaders actually displayed skills and plans without any training. It seems that their passion showed in an authentic way, and this passion transformed them into great orators when previously they could not speak, or into great leaders when before they were only administrators. This cannot be explained but only understood. Some others train their skills in anticipation of a calling. Transformational servant leaders train all their lives for that one moment when they are called, and then they find their true skill sets.

Transformational Servant Leaders See the Signals Amid the Noise

In electrical engineering and information technology, every learning brings noise (i.e., that which does not serve a purpose or have value but hinders the view of the truth in information). The signals are the key messages that are sent in any channel or are the result of any activity the corporation acts upon. Leaders can cut through the noise to find the core messages and determine which actions to take to drive change.

Transformational Servant Leaders Set Course and Believe

Carl Hammerschlag, author of *The Theft of the Spirit*, states, "If you stick to a plan without trying any of the byways, the end of the journey is just a place of preconception, not experience."[13]

He tells us that "mine was the arrogance that comes from certainty." Transformation has no certainty. We are trained to plan and to make all the checks and balances drive our success. Transformation has no guideposts, and the vision is less clear than operational plans. To transform to another form demands trust and instinct as well as a clear idea, but we are trained to tick and tie and remove ambiguity. In transformation, leaders must plan and work for removing ambiguity but also trust that what is to happen will happen; if they are right, things will fall into place. They must believe that what they are doing is for the greater good and not for their selfish regard.

Before we run with the notion that ambiguity, uncertainty, and everything soft is what transformational leaders do, remember that it takes a great deal of discipline and science to suspend beliefs and deal with truth as you can see it. It takes a greater discipline to understand what to fix and what to leave to time.

Steve Jobs stayed at Reed College in Portland, Oregon, as an official student for a very short time. He found it too expensive, so he dropped out. Staying with friends and sleeping on their floors, eating at the Hare Krishna temple, he decided to join a calligraphy class. Ten years later, the Macintosh was born with fonts. Steve Jobs believes that if he had not dropped out he would not have dropped in on the calligraphy class, and this would have created a chain reaction causing us not to have fonts in computers today.

Conditions That Bring Out Transformational Servant Leaders

Leaders seem to appear when there is need and respect for them. Transformational servant leaders await the inner opportunity to serve, and this powers them. There seems to be five preconditions, when satisfied, that bring leaders out to find their destiny. Business leaders and reformers of society share similar experiences.

Five Preconditions for Transformational Servant Leaders

The leaders' journey is often told simply. A person seems lost until a moment in which they see a conflict between their worldview and reality. They go through some sort of trauma, returning with great realization. From Moses to Mohammed, all great prophets lived through trauma. When trauma like this occurs, it unlocks leadership energies but this trauma causes a conflict between an established inner vision of reality and reality itself. We speak often of vision as the commodity of leaders. Vision is viewed as the sight of the mind. Leaders lead toward a direction, an objective, or a goal. Leadership is perceived primarily as directed action toward the achievement of an idea. Almost all great leaders did not start their lives knowing that they would lead. Maybe in the movies and storybooks, leader biographies give us the impression that all leaders plan for their moment in the sun. Research, however, proves that many leaders bumbled and staggered through life until certain forces, some external and others internal, collided.

The internal forces that forge leadership into the instruments of action help us understand whether leadership is inborn or learned, but inward events precede this outward action. Transformational servant leadership seems to be a result of the following five main forces colliding:

1. *Trauma and the leadership event.* This is the defined moment when a leader actually encounters suffering and chaos within. Here, questions challenge the leader. The power of the reality he or she sees forces him to understand that his vision is different than what is. He goes into a state of unacceptance and frustration.

2. *Awareness.* This is the critical transformation, a result of the collision of traumatic event and an inward dormant vision. Here the leader-to-be discovers that the trauma caused, in part, by reality is different from his inward vision of what can be. Realization visits when the leader transforms into a leader of his own beliefs rather than the instrument of others.

3. *Inward vision—the dream not communicated.* An inner dream, this is the dormant desire in any person to see life as he or she wishes. For Lincoln, it was to see a world in which slavery

was abolished. For Gandhi, it was respect and dignity for all. For Mandela, it was to end apartheid.

4. *Skills*. The tools for performing the task. One can debate whether skills can be learned or are a birthright.

5. *Plans*. Plans are structured methods to achieving the objectives. Leaders are dealers in hope, but they must put forth shrewd and sometimes cunning approaches to defeat their enemies. Leaders without action plans are warriors without weapons. Great leaders planned beyond their lifespan and never stopped planning. Walt Disney planned his next endeavor one day before his death. He never stopped building his castle in the sky.

Trauma and the Leadership Event

In Western societies we are taught to avoid trauma. We build systems to reduce trauma and to keep things calm. But many great things come from trauma. The first precondition to leadership is trauma. It is everywhere for us to take from it. Lee Bolman and Terrence Deal, authors of *Leading with Soul,* comment:

> History is full of stories of common people who do extraordinary things. In surmounting anguish and pain, they kindle their spirits and give strength to others. Our modern society encourages us to follow recipes or consult experts rather than find the fortitude to look inward.[14]

Trauma can strike anytime you dictate in society, but we run from it. Taken in context, trauma is healthy. It creates leaders or it creates victims. It shakes you up and rearranges your mental molecules. It makes us ask questions that are usually buried. Trauma does not always take dramatic form. In the case of Howard Schultz and Starbucks, it came in his visit to Europe as a coffee buyer who witnessed people sharing stories and enjoying coffee in outdoor cafes. This brought about his desire to bring that to the United States as a symbol of the need for society to gather.

Trauma to me might be different from trauma to you. For example, there are those who find airplane flights traumatic. Others find them an opportunity to read or relax. Some believe that losing your job (i.e., being fired) is disastrous, while others believe it provides opportunities for change. Two characters placed together represent "crisis" in Chinese. One is danger and the other is opportunity. The ancients believed that trauma was a source of energy, while we tend to remove crises as soon as we see them. In fact, we avoid it.

The world watched when Mohandas K. Gandhi fought the British not with knives and guns but with a nonviolent pen. He awakened the inner visions of 300 million Indians. These Indians separated after British rule to become Hindus and Muslims, who killed each other but stopped when Gandhi threatened to starve himself. If any politician decided to stop violence today by starving, would that stop anything? But this great man and great soul, the Mahatma, could hold the Indian world in his hands because they held his heart. So it may not be the act of leadership but the intent of leadership and the trust others have of this intent that powers leaders to create other transformational leaders.

Many leaders will share with you their moments of enlightenment, but they seldom come from enjoyable activities. Their leadership seems forged by trauma or in an event that shocks them into becoming more than they expected. Authors James Kouzes and Barry Posner, in *Encouraging the Heart*, declare:

> For aspiring leaders, this awakening initiates a period of intense exploration. A period of mixing and testing new ingredients; of invention; of going beyond technique; beyond training; beyond copying what the masters do, and beyond taking the advice of others. And if you surrender to it, after exhausting experimentation and often painful suffering you come to the third period. From all those abstract states on the canvas emerges and expression of self that is truly your own.[15]

Inward Vision: The Sight of the Mind

Leadership without vision can be disastrous. All the great leaders have communicated a vision. Common vision brings groups together. Vision is far too often equated with sharing vision with others, but transformational leaders attain inner vision before sharing it. But before this has to happen, leaders must isolate and understand their inner vision—what they believe deep inside. I call this the dream that never leaves you. We view the world a particular way, using this inner vision as a lens. From this place, we tend to dream of the possibilities. John F. Kennedy had a vision of America being the first on the moon. He shared this vision only after he decided its importance. He then put plans in place, removed mental barriers from his audience, and put the right talent in the right places.

A vision is a dream that never leaves you. It should awaken the very essence of your existence. Indirectly, a vision makes you, the transformed servant leader, what you are and what you can be.

Twentieth-century management teachings ask us to develop our vision through statements that can be shared and tested. They ask groups to share in this vision. They say that vision must be derivative of a rational process of evaluation and study. Too often we charge forward after a few whiteboard sessions without asking the deeper questions that engage our own inner energies, our life force, and the life force of our organizations. For Gandhi, the obvious disparateness in equality and equity in India got his inner vision to emerge. He discovered that his dream was "preservation of human dignity." For Lincoln, it was slavery that went counter to his inner being. Born in 1809 to a Kentucky farmer, Abraham Lincoln was one of seven children. He was a brooder, a loner, a melancholy man who many never expected to achieve anything. This was the case until he encountered his vision.

Inner, unshared vision is in all of us. Each of us unconscious leaders carries it to work and bury it with the "high-fat" low-impact deeds of the day. You may have seen people who move with conviction and who have an inspiration of what the future could be versus what is. Inner forces drive them to be far greater than the usual. Remember the last time you forgot that it was time to go to bed and worked because you wanted to see the result immediately, and you enjoyed every minute of creating it?

But even with this compulsion, these dreams can die inside mental fences. They are compelled to change the way of things, but their energies lose momentum when they confront the concrete walls of one's own mind. Their powerful visions become regrets of the past and nothing more. Someone once said that if you are about to die and someone else's life flashes by you, you know you've wasted your life! Many believe that not living your dream vision is the true sin in life.

Visions have certain undeniable characteristics:

- They are never completed and have built-in ambiguity. "Free the slaves" is compelling and controversial, but it's difficult to complete.
- Visions usually have metaphysical elements. Spiritual wheels powered many great leaders. Gandhi developed his vision of "nonviolent noncooperation" from reading the ancient Hindu text of the Bhagavad Gita and the Bible.
- Visions are proactive. They deal with transforming the way the world views something.
- Visions are not about you or your company but about the worldview after transformation occurs.
- Visions can be about a world that changes with action and about a new and vibrant ecosystem running under different paradigms of thought and action.
- Vision forms with or without your intervention. When you realize it, its work is done. Most of the time impatience kills vision before it can be self-sustaining, but vision is never wrong or right.
- Vision does not need skill or planning or structure. Skills are attained through effort and persistence. Vision is seldom attained through effort. Vision is realized from effort not due to effort.

Vision can die inside you every day. Carl Hammerschlag reminds us of this:

> I got older, I experienced failure, saw my hopes dashed, watched my doubt and cynicism grow until one day I only saw the way it was, not the way it might be. This is the ultimate blindness. This kind of blindness has got nothing to do with sight; it has to do with lack of vision, and vision is the stuff of dreams, hope and possibilities. Most of us scale down our dreams to the size of our fears until our vision becomes so tunneled we see darkness everywhere.[16]

Vision Can Transform an Organization One Person at a Time   Robert Quinn, author of *Deep Change*, states, "An organization also has an inner voice. Like the individual inner voice, it also calls for the continuous realignment of internal values and external realities." He further declares,

"The inner voice finds root in the moral core of the organization. When individual effort disconnects from the inner voice, people begin to lose vitality. Energy is lost. Human commitment begins to decay."[17] Early on, I declared that the principle of leadership and strategy are coming together and should not be in conflict when facing transformation in the market. Just as leaders face their inner demons and find the inner voice that propels them, organizations have an inner voice that propels them. In transformation, both are the same. When vision comes to each and every member of the organization, it becomes the fuel that propels the organization into action beyond any scorecard. Members of an organization know when they meet someone who has a practical vision and leads by example they tend to follow that vision.

Can a Vision Be Too Early for Action?   Sometimes when you miss a window of opportunity, you hit a wall of resistance. Bringing out your vision too early where it cannot breathe because critics can destroy the idea before facts are evident. If brought out too early, great visions may suffocate under the scrutiny from cynics.

The real challenge is to be patient with your dreams and not to remember them too often! In these days of documentation and being held accountable, it is a challenge to allow the leader to let go and assign a deep target to the intellect, not the ego. With ever-increasing bombardment of reporting and recording, we have not been permitted time to forget and partner with our insides in our leadership journeys. In these societies, bringing "things" to the surface, talking about them is the way to get them into action. But bringing things to the surface requires buoyancy of your ideas (i.e., they must be ready to take flight). Time must wait for the vision to develop. Maybe we should nurture our dreams and let them incubate for a while. Inner vision takes a longer time to form. We live in an uncompromising world that expects any problem to be introduced and solved within 60 minutes with four commercial breaks. Leaders who have a vision are patient with their ideas and plan for success.

Skills and Plans to Transform—Born or Made?

Notice that anyone who encounters trauma and shakes his or her inner vision into focus has not satisfied all the preconditions for leadership. This argument will not deny the need for skills. Leaders have trained themselves for the great leadership moment or skills have just burst out of them after the other preconditions were internalized. True realization almost transforms the mere mental molecular structure of the leader, enough so that what remains is a different and highly developed person. One can argue that the leader gains skills in anticipation, but most transformational servant leaders were not packaging their skills in anticipation of the unanticipated. They encountered a strong force or forces, found their true calling, and then quite suddenly became different people with more accentuated skills to deliver to the task at hand. But if we are to examine leadership in general, we cannot count on forces forging our skills. We must build our awareness of these conditions and practice these conditions in the work laboratory.

We cannot explain how leaders who find themselves and their true calling suddenly perform all the skills that they could not muster before. I have witnessed the recipe forming in teammates who I have led into their leadership. They feel the trauma of the demands to lead, so they run to the skill playbooks and find techniques as their anchor; these fail to win also. Then they introspect, trying to find the why in what they do and for whom. As they discover a love greater than the love of wealth, fame, and themselves and uncover a greater good that pulls them rather than fear that pushes them, they find their confidence because it is for others, not themselves.

They transform themselves, caring less of what others want but more about what they believe truth is. Powered by this, they cultivate their skills and develop techniques to manage their plans to the target with an eye to the cause they serve.

Transformational servant leaders train on skills and are introspective to prepare for the leadership moment that they are destined to discover. Some also bumble their way through life with experiences that only seem disconnected until shock and trauma visit them. Then everything comes together to form the reason for them to lead.

Do You Work in a Kingdom or a Corporation?

Are organizations ready to be led this way? With all these centuries of skill-based alignment and service-averse management, employees have been trained to follow the hierarchical power base. They are now living in disguise, resisting change because they actually disrespect you if you do not behave like John Wayne riding into a den of the enemy with only one gun! Under this severe mental inertia of the teams, self-leadership could die instantly.

Under the guise of being an incorporated entity, some corporations function like a kingdom. A kingdom responds in the following way:

- Power is the currency of the land.
- She who has land has power. Territory and budget drive your blast zone of power.
- Anger the king or the people who influence the king and you die.
- Pleasing the king and the key influencers who whisper in the king's ear is the way to win.
- Loyalty is proven when you do what the king and his influencers tell you to do.
- Don't show weakness or vulnerability or a challenging opinion, or you will be killed.
- Make it the king's idea if you are right, make it your idea when it is wrong, and you will be spared this round.
- The last person to influence the king wins because he is highly influenced by the last idea.
- Beware the king's heir because he is looking for who will usurp the king. Know when to side with him or be killed when power transfers.
- Subjects are to be commanded, not lead or cherished, because you show weakness in caring. If you have your own army's loyalty, you could think about challenging the king.
- The king answers to no one.

Corporations are reputed to be about:

- Merit is the basis of promotion and rank is not.
- Influence is a stronger currency to getting things done over power.
- Market dominance and not politics in the workplace.
- Leading and managing work more effectively compared to commanding.
- The CEO is more interested in authenticity than in who has power over his future.

- The CEO listens to the right voice, not the same voice.
- The CEO is a leader but is also a follower of a purpose greater than him or her.
- Politics is not the key driver of the market machinery because in the end, customers don't purchase politics; they purchase a vision and products that live to that vision.
- Communities are inside the corporation and also outside as customers. They relate to one another as one cohesive but different set of ideals and ideas.
- The king answers to the board, and they both answer to the general public who are stakeholders in the community asset.

These traits are not meant to be exact. They are perceptions and should be taken as such. However, organizations function with traits from both of these lists and leadership in such organizations can be confusing.

Can Transformational Servant Leadership Work in a Kingdom?

Some people are so "damaged" from their work relationships that they can't see the forest for the trees. Their pain is so high and their fear is so like a siren that they are always reacting. How can trans-formational leaders assist them when they cannot see themselves? The only help you can offer is to stand your ground, not chase them into oblivion, and not make them feel better because you are feeding their fear. Never try to explain to them that things will get better and more defined, because you really don't know that. The only way out is found inside them, but only they can travel this path.

The problem is exaggerated because the organizations of today have developed systems and methodologies based on protection rather than protection and progression. Systems are put in place to catch, correct, and function with the lowest common denominator in mind. More systems retain than pertain to the generative employee. More forms, regulations, and policies protect rather than promote. It is as if we built a castle and imprisoned our best! These are very necessary practices but if it becomes the organization's personality, then transformation will tend to not take root.

Besides the organization's systems, there are those among us who believe that the status quo is best. If that person or persons are the ones in authority, then transformation will take a back seat to status quo. What is a status quo leader like? He manages by an outward facade of thoughtful concern for his people but is self-driven. In fact, he sees himself to be giving his people protection while he is growing them slowly (because they are not ready!). He is constantly pushing them down to ensure that he is still the leader and will protect his power base. He is a master at managerial manipulation and is highly schooled. He empowers and believes that giving power to others requires controls on them to justify his existence. He does not believe that there may be another way and works from a dream that is already over. His horizon of possibilities is right below his nose, so he calls himself practical. He sees no possibilities, just practicalities. He is articulate and well formed in his thinking, basing all his comments in calculations of today that regress to tomorrow because today is tomorrow with him leading in his mind. He will subdue his thinking only if you are more powerful, but he will listen to you because he wants to know how to subdue you rather than learn. He is jealous of your and others' skills because that is how he wants to win. He uses humor but is not humorous. He uses trust to mean consistency because to him consistency is being trustworthy. Ambiguity is his enemy because predictability is his weapon.

Can transformational servant leaders work in a kingdom? Yes. Most autocratic organizations are ripe for transformational leadership. I do not judge one form of leadership from another but in this new era where transformation awaits business markets, we need leaders who can see themselves in a new world. In fact, the best leaders for transformation are ones who want to fire themselves from the status quo so that they can get hired by the future.

Diary of a Transformational Servant Leader

Legendary leader Brad Anderson is the former CEO and vice chairman of Best Buy.

He is humble but a true transformative leader. Under his leadership Best Buy grew from a small establishment to the number one consumer electronics retailer in the United States.

He is an authentic leader and very skilled in strategy and leadership.

The Formative Years

He was born in 1949 in Sheridan, Wyoming, the oldest child in his family. He admits he was at best a C student. He loves music of all sorts, history, and most of all biographies. He joined the Sound of Music, a small chain of music stores, in 1973.[18]

The Leadership Event

In 1979 Anderson met Richard Schulze, the CEO and founder of the store. Schulze asks Anderson to meet him outside the store, and Anderson believes he is going to be fired. Instead, Schulze asks his advice on whom to promote. Anderson decides to ask for the opportunity. He believes that when things are at their toughest, you have the freedom of it being so. He also believed that he was the person to take the company forward. His leadership style was intentionally to destabilize the environment because he was the driver of transformation. He reminds us those leaders often forget why they are leading and then place their own interests above the responsibility to lead. Anderson saw it as his role to not let that happen.

Customer Centricity

He was always customer focused and found value in what the customers wanted. He watched the shopping patterns of the community.

He drove that into a competency of the company. Anderson was looking for the unique insight that people are having with their connection with his stores.

His insight into customers came from traveling around and speaking with big thinkers like Larry Selden, a professor at Columbia Business School. Such encounters brought him concepts like customer centricity. Other ideas, like noncommissioned sales personnel, were challenged, but he persisted to form a new way to sell electronics products. Brad redesigned the habits of sales and gave them salaries so they would focus on the customer and not the commission. Brian Dunn, then COO, tried to convince him to stop this model but Anderson declared that he should think about the next fifteen years, not the next five years.

Anderson never forgot his role as transformational leader. He knew that transformation demands humility and that it is not about himself but about the core values in action. He declared that you are part of the story and at times you may be in the way of the story showing his understanding of his role as a leader.

Anderson is keenly self-aware and was a strong reason for the success of Best Buy. He is an example of a leader who transformed for the sake of a cause to bring value to his customers and in the process affected society.

Summary and Observations

Transformational servant leaders are the foundation of a transformed market. They power the transformation of any organization, and they can come from the customers or from the employees. They are powered by a desire to serve others, and they forget themselves, and this is the source of their undying energy and success. They do not come to this easily but through self-doubt, suffering, ridicule, and even pain. Yet they are among us and we should realize that we cannot judge anyone in our organization to be inadequate, of not having ideas to transform the world around them. Our purpose is to nurture and to find the goose that lays the golden eggs rather than be in the business of ideas. Be in the business of nurturing people with ideas, and the ideas will flow.

Transformational leaders base their actions on their beliefs and they discover causes. When markets transform and when you want the company to understand and lead the preparation for transformation, you need transformed leaders who can see the need and can gather the customers and employees in this preparation. Lessons come from great transformative leaders in our society as well as great entrepreneurs but they display similar traits.

The internal forces that forge leadership into the instruments of action help us understand if leadership is inborn or learned. But inward events precede this outward action. This event is a result of the following five main forces colliding. So leaders are actually born and made by five forces that bring out the best in them when the time and place are aligned for action toward a transformation:

1. Trauma and the leadership event
2. Awareness
3. Inward vision—the dream not communicated
4. Skills
5. Plans

Notes

1   Max DePree, *Leadership is an Art* (New York: Doubleday, 2004).
2   Carol M. Orsborn, *Inner Excellence at Work: The Path to Meaning, Spirit, and Success* (Amacom, 1999).
3   Robert K. Greenleaf, *The Servant-Leader Within: A Transformative Path* (New Jersey: Paulist Press, 2003), p. 68.
4   Eknath Easwaran, *Gandhi the Man: The Story of His Transformation* (Petaluma, CA: Nilgiri Press, 1972), p. 53.
5   Greenleaf, *The Servant-Leader Within: A Transformative Path* (New Jersey: Paulist Press, 2003), p. 68.
6   Nikos Mourkogiannis, *Purpose: The Starting Point of Great Companies* (New York: Palgrave Macmillan, 2006), p. 20.
7   Easwaran, *Gandhi the Man: The Story of His Transformation* (Petaluma, CA: Nilgiri Press, 1972), p. 41.
8   Ibid.
9   Abraham Zaleznik, *The Managerial Mystique: Restoring Leadership in Business* (New York: Harper and Row, 1989).
10 Zaleznik, *The Managerial Mystique*, p. 257.
11 Easwaran, *Gandhi the Man*, p. 64.
12 DePree, *Leadership Is an Art*.
13 Carl A. Hammerschlag, *Theft of the Spirit: A Journey to Spiritual Healing* (New York: Simon & Schuster, 1970), p. 43.
14 Lee G. Bolman and Terrence E. Deal, *Leading with Soul: An Uncommon Journey of Spirit* (San Francisco: Jossey-Bass, 1995), p. 59.
15 James M. Kouzes and Barry Z. Posner, *Encouraging the Heart: A Leader's Guide to Rewarding and Recognizing Others* (San Francisco: Jossey-Bass, 2003), p. 148.
16 Hammerschlag, *Theft of the Spirit*, p. 100.
17 Robert E. Quinn, *Deep Change: Discovering the Leader Within* (San Francisco: Jossey-Bass, 1996), p. 201.
18 Mathew Boyle, "Best Buy's Giant Gamble," *Fortune*, March 29, 2006. http://money.cnn.com/magazines/fortune/fortune_archive/2006/04/03/8373034/index.htm

CHAPTER 8

Sin #6: Mistaking Capability for Strategic Competency

Many executives lock themselves in conference rooms or resort hotel rooms to uncover their organizational strategy. That is a good thing. But strategy formulated with little regard to the strengths and weaknesses in capability is blind strategy. The true power of strategy can only be expressed in work performed. Hence, the real challenge seems to be not only strategy formulation, but also the ability to create an operational framework to execute the strategy and the ability to achieve the goal consistently and successfully for as long as it takes. This is competence. While capability is about what you can do, competence is about the recipe of your capabilities and what you can do better than others consistently as far as your customers perceive.

In transforming times, how does one succeed doing things better than others when what they do better than others may no longer be of value to customers? How does a corporation change its basic core competence to meet market demands? Well, that is difficult but possible. When we think of capabilities, we can acquire or divest in our capability but to divest or build a new competence, the recipe that makes you who you are to customers is far more challenging.

If we only know how to build big vehicles and the market wants small vehicles, how do we get there from here? Then, should we change so dramatically by firing our capabilities and buying new ones?

As you know, business is about change. Change has affected business models dramatically over the years. Mergers and acquisitions can transform the landscape as power shifts between companies who gain capability as well as competences.

Strategy as a Portfolio of Competencies

C. K. Prahalad and Gary Hamel, noted authors and thought leaders, declared that large businesses ran themselves as a portfolio of businesses rather than a portfolio of competencies. For example, Sony has a mission of building advanced technologies and innovation in the marketplace.[1] Their competency seems to be in making electronics smaller—miniaturization.[2] Similarly, 3M Corporation makes products, but what it does best is adhesive products.[3] Strategy can be defined as the unique, differentiating value to the customer that is found in the personality and learned behaviors of the organization. In this definition, strategy can be the way the corporation builds and sells products and services. Identifying and exploiting these competencies is the challenge. New industries can be discovered if corporations can predict the competencies of future target markets and build them. Corporations that set out to identify future momentum drivers and isolate future necessitating competencies stand a better chance to win.

Competencies play a significant role in strategy formulation because they ground the planning phase with a reality check by asking the following questions:

- Can we accomplish these grand dreams if we cannot execute them due to the unique skills and learning within the organization?
- Do we have to and can we acquire skills and learning to attend to the changing market demands?
- Who else can step up and deliver value with lasting competencies?

Identifying, Isolating, and Enabling Core Competencies

First of all, competencies come in two flavors:

1. *First-order competencies.* These are the skills and capabilities within the company that, if organized well, provide a strong,

competitive advantage in the marketplace. The recipe of this mix is key in delivering true value to the target customers. For example, Southwest Airlines has isolated and exploited the key value proposition in its customers that the larger carriers essentially noted but did not serve. Customers wanted a way to fly short hauls and not worry about losing bags and so on. They wanted to fly inexpensively but were willing to give up luxuries like food and assigned seating. In return they would like to get out on time and get to their destination on time. They also knew that flying was a hassle and that a fun airline to fly did not mean that the airline did not take flying seriously. It is in this carefully constructed value proposition that Southwest Airlines opened the skies to many nonflyers.

2. *Second-order competency.* This works in concert with the unique combination or recipe of activities that form the center of the value proposition to the customer. This competency is an overriding personality that an organization portrays to its customers and within the company. Consider the prior discussion about Sony and how whatever they seem to do, they make things smaller.

The combination of both of these defined competencies forms the basis for whether strategy can be realized. Without capability and uniqueness in business design, strategy is nothing more than a word.

Understanding your competencies is not enough. Knowing them in the context of your value to customers and in the context of the market transformation is essential. Furthermore, a competence is not one activity but a set of skills and technologies, business processes, and practices held together by a cause. Competence creates value that customers want and are willing to purchase regularly.

For companies to transform their competencies, they must have as much ability to change their strategy as to formulate one. This is characterized by several core abilities:

- The ability to connect the cause of their institution to the work done.
- The ability to formulate strategic thrusts or theme (i.e., several key strategic objectives to focus the organization for the next 5 to 10 years).
- The ability to institutionalize and operationalize these thrusts into key management objectives and measures.

- The ability to translate these objectives to key activities and combination of activities that produce the desired outcomes and outputs (i.e., the ability to adapt these activities to what the market demands).

Difference between Recipe (Competency) and Ingredient (Capability)

3M's focus is to solve problems with innovation. Among other things, what 3M does well is innovate. This is a capability. But how it innovates and how it defines a recipe to the customer, that is a competence. Nike's focus seems to be about competitiveness and innovative products. Nike designs and produces shoes and apparel. That is capability. The way it refines its capabilities into a value to the customers who feel that they are buying innovation and competitiveness is called competence. Sony believes that customers want to experience the joy of applying technology to the benefit of people. Walmart began with Sam Walton, who wanted to give ordinary people the opportunity to purchase the same things that better-off people can. Nordstrom believes in heroic customer service. All these organizations linked their core purpose and philosophy to the actual work done every day. The work done at the levels that touch the customers is designed to reflect this core belief, or cause, and express this core belief to the customer.

The difference between a recipe and ingredient is the difference between eating at my house when I cook and when you go to dinner at a good restaurant. We both used the same ingredients, but somehow the resulting output and outcome are far apart. Organizations can hire similar skilled people and do similar work with similar measures but have radically different outcomes. That is possibly why the Toyota production system is difficult to replicate well in the United States.

A recipe is what great organizations strive for. In transformational climates, linear approaches to capability are short lived. If you believe that being good at one key capability is sufficient, you had best make sure that it is nonreplicable. Winning, using competencies, is more about combining the following ingredients:

- Creating brand awareness among your customers and prospects who feel an alignment between the organization and their values.

- Defining communicable cause/purpose that is about a transformed customer and experience with that customer.
- Combining key ingredients that reflect a valued recipe that creates a strong, enduring, and authentic "aftertaste" to the customer, who keeps returning because of it.
- Creating a structure that drives social networked feedback interactively with an approachable organizational culture.

Finding the Positive "Aftertaste" for Customers

In the past, we all agreed that we should pick one thing we do well (e.g., we innovate, or we are customer intimate, or we are efficient/effective). We believe that this focus will define us just as it has defined Starbucks, Nordstrom, and so on. Michael Treacy and Fred Wiersema, authors of *The Discipline of Market Leaders*, list three strategic thrusts to market leaders:

1. Operational excellence
2. Product leadership
3. Customer intimacy[4]

They argued that companies that succeeded had chosen one of these three dimensions to lead in. Focus meant that we would have to choose one of these axes and build our company on this focus. Many companies have become great with such focus, but transformational organizations take it one more level.

Innovative Intimacy

Apple did not win markets by being innovative. Apple transformed the market using innovative products that consumers now believe is intimate to their lives. Many competitors are not able to catch up with the iPad with respect to price because Apple has mastered the art of building them effectively and efficiently. Consumers live with their iPods, iPhones, and iPads, and they believe that these products represent their unique signature of their personalities. In a sense, Apple has defined innovation and intimacy as its signature. It has transformed the consumer experience with computers and ubiquitous devices. The future may be bright for all the competitors who pursue this format for competitiveness, but

Apple created the pathway with its unique capabilities combined into competence.

USAA, the financial service institution dedicated to the nation's military families, has also innovated on direct marketing and pioneered using the Internet and phones sales to create an intimate relationship with clients. Customers take advice from the sales associates and believe they are in a unique club of 7.4 million members.

Tom Vaugh, director of social media at USAA, states:

> As we improve these relationships, members will tell even more of their friends and family about how much they trust USAA—continuing our history of growth via word-of-mouth.[5]

This further exemplifies how innovation and intimacy work in concert to be competencies of leading organizations. One can argue that these organizations are still focused on one key aspect and using other enablers to give them lift (e.g., Apple is an innovative company but has developed an intimacy-driven user interface).

Efficient Innovation

3M has built a business on innovation and has made it efficient as a process. Unlike many other organizations that spark innovative ideas, 3M has designed and executed on a corporate philosophy in action to build assets that are constantly applied to innovative solutions for everyday life. Using a large number of technical platforms almost like a periodic table of technology assets, 3M directs these technologies onto areas of everyday life from stop signs to teeth whitening. The 3M innovation center is a must-visit site for any team that wants to understand the industrialization of innovation. Founded as the Minnesota Mining and Manufacturing Company, bringing about the delivery of sandpaper, Scotch Tape, masking tape, and the famous Post-it note, 3M is the strong example of efficient innovation. The basis of its innovation is its people. 3M calls it the 15 percent rule. 3M encourages its scientists to spend 15 percent of their work week playing and experimenting on ideas they are interested in. This opens ups opportunities for new ideas and innovation.[6]

Efficient Intimacy

Best Buy has attempted to optimize intimacy to the customer. From noncommissioned customer sales to its quick-response Geek Squad, customers know they will receive predictable, efficient, and timely service.

Starbucks has also mastered the art of efficient intimacy by providing a perceived endless choice of beverages with a brand that stands for service. Like Dell, Starbucks sends a message of personalization (i.e., have it your way), when actually it has identified the needs of its customers and formulated a way to provide beverages and food to customers who believe that they are ordering off the menu:

> Starbucks provides an excellent example of the deft handling of capability variability. The coffee shop allows customers to choose among many permutations of sizes, flavor, and preparation techniques in its beverages. In the interests of filing orders accurately and efficiently, Starbucks trains its counter clerks to call out orders to beverage makers in a particular sequence.[7]

Starbucks has the capability to service a variety of customer needs while keeping the customer feeling personally served. This can be described as "mass customization." I prefer to call it efficient intimacy, because there is nothing mass about the customer experience at Starbucks; it is intimate and scalable. Mass customization is a capability, not a competence. Customization is the art and science of delivery to the customer, but the experience the customer gains is found in the unique recipe delivered by the organization that designs this into its recipe.

Key Capabilities for Transforming Markets

I have spent the first quarter of this chapter speaking of competence as a recipe. But we cannot view capability as subordinate to competence. Capabilities are key ingredients to competence. Furthermore, leading organizations are also transforming capability to address transforming markets. Three capabilities are important in many transforming markets:

1. Innovation
2. Partnering
3. Social media

Innovation

In new markets formed from transformation, innovation plays a significant role in identifying new solutions to customers who develop new needs. "In the future, the real core competence of companies will be the ability to continuously and creatively destroy and remake themselves to meet customer demands," states leadership expert Noel Tichey.[8] The romance around innovation makes it even more challenging to describe and diagnose. In many ways, the word has lost its meaningfulness because it is all things to all people. Innovation and invention are used synonymously, but they are not always the same.

Invention is the creation of something unique; *innovation* is the assembling or assimilation of several inventions and/or other items to form a new offering. Coffee, living rooms, baristas, and unique consumer experience existed before Starbucks, but now they are all ingredients in the Starbucks recipe for customers. The unique offering of innovation and how it is nurtured, understood, and engaged in organizations determine the organization's leadership characteristics in transformation. Those who rely on efficiency and intimacy without innovating in these areas can fall behind.

Where Are Transformative Ideas Born?   Ideas executed well fuel innovation. But how do we spark innovative ideas in markets where the unknown unknowns are so much greater than the known unknowns? Are they all born from a lightning bolt in our brains? Or are new thoughts just coincidence? Steven Johnson, author of *Where Good Ideas Come From*, believes a 10/10 rule applies to ideas—10 years to build and 10 years for it to hit a mass audience.[9] He cited the VCR to HDTV to debunk the current expectation that ideas implemented can grow like Facebook and PayPal, which grew relatively quickly in revenues. He identifies four ways to think of ideas being born:

1. *Adjacency*—looking for one idea that is next to another and so on.
2. *Liquid networks*—connections in our brains manufacture ideas and reconfigure old ones.

3. *Slow hunch*—it takes time to make connections.
4. *Serendipity*—the concept of unlikely collisions and discoveries.

Johnson argues that these four foundational approaches create ideas:

> You can see the fingerprints of the adjacent possible in one of the most remarkable patterns in all the intellectual history, what scholars now call "the multiple": A brilliant idea occurs to a scientist or inventor somewhere in the world, and he goes public with his remarkable finding, only to discover that three other minds had independently come up with the same idea in the past year.[10]

He notes that a good idea is a network. "A specific constellation of neurons—thousands of them—fire in sync with each other for the first time in your brain and an idea pops into your consciousness."[11] Johnson explains that connections in densely populated relationships form and reconfigure into ideas in our brains and in our communities. He is not supportive of the collective brain concept where the group is better than the individual thought. Actually, he declares that "it is not that the network is smart; it's that the individuals get smarter because they're connected to the network."[12] He explains that ideas don't come from labs but from places where people gather to present their ideas. Hence, "ground zero of innovation was not the microscope. It was the conference table."[13]

Ideas are found in places of contemplation like walks, showers, and other places where we rest and reconnect. The coincidence may not be so coincidental after all. Tom Kelley, general manager of IDEO, a leading design company and author of *The Art of Innovation*, supports this notion of collaboration and experimentation and serendipity using "quick prototyping" to create the elements of coincidence.

"Quick prototyping is about acting before you've got the answers, about taking chances, stumbling a little, but then making it right."[14] He says, "Prototyping doesn't just solve straight forward problems. Call it serendipity or even luck, but once you start drawing or making things, you open up new possibilities of discovery."[15]

So, innovation is about comfort in ambiguity and comfort with seemingly disconnected ideas and thoughts. This is somewhat unnatural for adults but completely natural for children, who have not yet escaped the world of possibilities and dreams.

Conflicting Expectations Create Innovative Ideas   AdAge.com ranks the slogan "Tastes great less filling" number four of the 10 best slogans of the century.[16] Miller Lite advertising promoted this slogan to represent conflicting expectations of their customers. Some believed that to have a light beer, one must sacrifice taste. Miller decided to tell the audience that they could have both, thus framing a new market.

The central theme behind this example is that innovative ideas are not always born in connections of commonality or adjacency but that conflicting demands may create a new ideas or concepts. Conflicting concepts, if brought together, can be the basis for an innovation idea. Consider the assumption that small cars are uncomfortable. Honda Civic brought the concept of small into the United States in 1972. Starting small with limited features, the Civic has now become a symbol of comfort. In earlier years, comfort meant large vehicles with options. Today, comfort has been redefined for many people to mean economical and shapely.

The place to seek innovative ideas is in conflicting areas where two or three concepts of assumptions don't seem to get along. For example, travelers are resigned to the notion that their bags may be lost or misdirected when they fly. The assumption is that you have no control over your own bags and you will never know whether you'll have them until you see them again. If we think of bags like packages we send, we should know where they are at any time, especially if they are on the same airplane. How about allowing consumers and travelers to have the basic knowledge that their bags are on the same airplane just minutes before their flight? Would you pay for that service? Could a device be embedded in every bag so that it tells you it is near you?

Innovators Create Coincidence   Some believe that coincidence is the accidental connections that occur to individuals and groups. Others believe that divine intervention causes these seemingly random and unlikely connections and events that trigger ideation.

Innovators know that these connections can be organized or stimulated into being. Coincidences happen every day if you notice. It is a coincidence if you expected rain, brought an umbrella, and it actually rained. Yet, that is viewed as being prepared. One can be prepared, trained, and ready for coincidence so that one can take full advantage of it when it arrives.

If we were walking with Howard Schultz when he had his epiphany about creating customer experience while he watched others gathering in a café, would we have had a similar insight?

Strategic Capability of Innovation and Implementing Ideas   Innovation is not about ideas but about ideas that are implemented by people, ideas that can produce revenue, margins, and impact society. Innovation is about people with implementable ideas. It starts with elegant insight, and then this insight is forced into place using decades of thinking, feeling, researching, and observing. Transformative companies nurture people (not ideas) and enable them to create the future.

Noel M. Tichy, author of *The Leadership Engine*, asserts, "The world is moving too quickly for bureaucratic caretakers to stay on top" and "success in the new global marketplace requires constant innovation, redeployment of resources and risk."[17] Carved into value propositions that focus on specific target customers and segments, this idea takes flight backed by a model of what and who the customer is; it is a business model and a financial model.

Efficiency or Innovation?   Of efficiency and innovation, which is core to transformation? Both are. Without the operational part, organizations cannot power themselves through any transformation. Without innovation, efficiency cannot drive organizations forward. Vijay Govindarajan, noted author and educator on innovation, has declared that innovation cannot be separated from the workings of the organization. Yet, innovation and efficiency of the existing organization are sometimes viewed as opposites, especially when it comes to budgets and where money should be invested. Hence, innovation tends to be prioritized against efficiency. Govindarajan advocates that the innovation enterprise should partner with what he calls the "performance engine" to signify the operational parts of the organization whose focus is effective/efficient repeatable output. Innovation engines are equally focused on efficiency but approach it in a different way. Innovation engines, if we may so call the organizations focused on disruptive innovation, are focused on nonlinear approaches to creating their output. They can run sometimes without a defined outcome, hovering over ideas rather than formulating solutions like a production system. Innovation engine teams visit and revisit the same ideas over and over. Contemplation is the key element of exploration and innovation in its early stages.

Transformative organizations know how to meld both these different approaches to problem solving (i.e., one to improve incrementally and the other to find new and disruptive solutions into the organization's personality). Before we leave with the idea that innovation is less disciplined than the efficient operational part of the organization, let us consider Professor Govindarajan's insights:

> Though innovation must be evaluated differently, there is no reason that innovators cannot be every bit as disciplined and accountable as the performance engine.
>
> Many of the fundamental principles for managing an innovation initiative bear little resemblance to the fundamental principles for managing the performance engine.[18]

Govindarajan has developed superb documentation on the fundamental differences between the organization charged with sustainment and the organization charged with innovation. He continues:

> At the same time, the greatest strength of a Performance Engine— its drive for repeatability and predictability—also establishes its greatest limitations. By definition, innovation is neither repeatable nor predictable. It is exactly the opposite—no routine and uncertain. These are fundamental incompatibilities between innovation and ongoing operations.[19]

These two necessary parts of the future need different leadership styles, operating processes, and most of all, cultures for growth. Clayton Christensen also has established principles of disruptive innovation and what larger institutions must guard against. In *The Innovator's Dilemma,* he states:

> Sustaining projects addressing the needs of the firms' most powerful customers almost always preempt resources from disruptive technologies with small markets and poorly defined customer needs.[20]

Innovations are about continuous change in market needs and redefinition as organizations uncover the changing needs of future customers, while sustaining a business is about consistently and predictably providing incremental value to the current customers in current markets.

> Typically when performance fails short of plan, these systems encourage management to close the gap between what was planned, and what happened, that is, they focus on unanticipated failures.[21]

In transformation, organizations find it difficult to anticipate failure because markets are shifting and new demands appear. It requires organizations to anticipate, sometimes test, and most times to guess possible unique solutions to new customer challenges. This is different from finding gaps and closing them in an incremental exercise such as asking the customer what is difficult and fixing it. In transformation, many times the customer does not yet know what the gaps are because the market has yet to shift.

Partnering

Organizations lose their way by assembling the wrong combination of competencies to achieve future growth. Once we pick the wrong direction, we are dead from the start. If we pick the right direction but assemble incongruent capabilities, it would be very expensive to retrace the path taken with the wrong talent or skill base.

There are four ways (four Bs) organizations can look at partnerships in a transformative market:

1. *Buy*—acquire the organization that exemplifies the competency or market share for the future markets.
2. *Build*—take the challenge of designing and building a unique offering or infrastructure for the future. This may take more time to do.
3. *Borrow*—partner tightly or loosely with other players in the ecosystem to gain access to a capability that you may not want to purchase or build.
4. *Bury*—you can just downplay the importance of this offering that is currently in the market. Use your market might to debunk this capability to devalue it.

How do you know when and how to do any of these things in a market about to transform? Let us assume that you have already

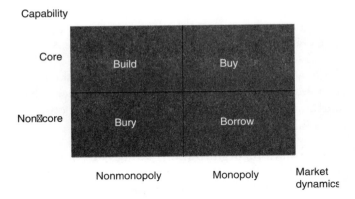

Exhibit 8.1   Partnership Decision Matrix

identified that the offering or business you observe has capabilities that target customers in a transformed environment will value. Exhibit 8.1 illustrates the four possible actions an organization can take along two critical axes of considerations:

1. Is the capability or company you are assessing in a market where it is considered a monopoly, where no one else has a competitive offering, or are there options?
2. Is this capability core to your new capabilities, or is it not core to your future?

If the business or capability is core to your future but there are many who offer this, consider that you can either build it if you have the range of time and talent or purchase the capacity through acquisitions. Exhibit 8.1 places these considerations in a decision matrix. Organizations have many variables to consider, such as:

- Can we build it?
- What is unique about our offering compared with others?
- If there are many in the market with this capability, maybe an insignificant acquisition might jump-start the project.

If the capability is not core to the business and there are many in the market players, why not just make it insignificant as a comparative advantage? Unless the movements in the market are to consolidate assets, consider an ignore strategy.

If the business alliance forms a core part of your business asset, but there are only a few in the market that own that asset, consider an outright acquisition. The price may be high because of the monopolistic nature of the offering, and you might decide it is not an option. A build option, or a build after a few purchases, might be appropriate.

If the capability you seek is not core to you but necessary and the market has only one place that offers you the solution, you would best strike an alliance with the entity while considering the following:

- Consider that the entity you ally with will become more market powerful with this capability because of your acknowledgement and subtle endorsement.
- If so, the market may believe that that your ally is more important than it really is.
- Why not try to encourage others to build this capability by coinvesting so that the monopoly does not turn against you? For example, if you signed a partnership with the entity, what if your competitors acquired it?

The four Bs are only a guide, and not a rulebook, to partnership strategies. Many organizations have formal departments that focus on alliances. This may be appropriate in transformative times, since the market power of large incumbents flattens when small companies may have the same influence as the incumbents. At such a time, transformative organizations focus all their assets to gain power with their competencies while guarding the current market that they dominate.

Time is an important variable in your considerations, namely, do you have time to build? Exhibit 8.1 is a very simple model with a complex set of considerations. However, you can use this model to give you a starting point and help you keep boundaries to your options before you act with the vast amount of information and teams you may bring to bear on this question of how you partner in preparation for transformation.

The business world is riddled with successes and failures from partnerships that range from joint ventures to acquisitions. Many books have been written on the "right" way to do this. I shall not go into those ways or provide a compendium of the options. However, there is much to be learned from the nature of these partnerships. Many times, these partnerships fail for less obvious reasons than given. For example, it is believed that how we go into a partnership defines its outcomes. Our organizational attitude and altitude must be understood. Organizations have an attitude about alliances. Some do it as a power move, while others see it as a sharing of power (i.e., a sharing of an open philosophy). Some fly at a strategic altitude for alliances (i.e., they justify what imperative or initiative the current alliance serves before anything is attempted). Others like small acquisitions. Experienced alliance builders know the art of the deal, and they think both short and long term. They understand that the technical aspect of an alliance is one half of the equation and that alliances also depend on self-awareness. In other words, if you plan to partner, you, not the other guy, are anchor to the success or failure.

Social Media

Frank Eliason is the most famous customer service manager in the United States.[22] He is Comcast's "Twitter man" because he came up with the idea to "tweet" customers of Comcast after searching the Web for any mention of Comcast in a negative way.

With only two and a half years under his belt, he became the director of digital care and set the pace for corporations to follow into the social media revolution. It used to be that one person could not bring down a nation, or at least it took decades to do so. Now, revolutions can bring down a nation in weeks with social media behind the people. The voice of one can change the entire balance of power in the world.

Social media includes YouTube, Twitter, and Facebook, to mention a few. Some are business networks, and others are narcissistic destinations where users chest beat or write posts about their indulgences. Social media can be described as tools that are online where content, opinions, perspectives, insights, and media are shared with other people. Some people create content, while others lurk, observe, or disseminate the material. At its core, social media is about relationships and connections between people and organizations. Social media is new to the business world, but social interactions are not. It is part of our DNA. We are all experimenting, so anyone who pretends to be expert in these topics is ignorant, rare, or audacious.

Should We Consider Social Media in Transformation? Yes, we should consider social media a tool of transformation, but we should not start our social media strategy by measuring its value up front because social media is about the way in which people communicate, just like the telephone. Businesses issue phones to their key employees all the time but do not ask them to justify the value of the phone, because immediate access to work and communications is an essential part of the character of business. Social media is similar.

When we deploy such new approaches, we are first trying to find value in the technology and approach, and experimentation is key. We see many unique uses of social media, but when you start, you should first look for the direction it takes you, not measure if you got there.

Social media in organizations is actually organizational transformation using social media. People in organizations are talking to each other inside and outside the company at a scale that is unknown to our current-state organizations.

Diversity in Social Media Blogs, mashups, podcasts, widgets, wikis, and vlogs (video logs) are all different expressions of social media. Each has significance to the virtual world and serves different purposes. In a rough sense, they all work in concert to create the experience on the Internet:

- *Blogs.* Users post messages in an attempt to start a conversation or debate.
- *Mashup.* Web site or property that brings together various information sources and creates a unique offering with this information.
- *Widgets.* Piece of software that performs a task of some sort on the Web.
- *Wiki.* Piece of software or content that allows for group collaboration and editing. Usually found in "wiki" pages that define a topic of interest that is edited and created by many users.
- *Vlogs.* Video logs as in YouTube.com.
- *Twitter.* Speaking to others in short timely phrases.

Social media is the variety of media offerings that surround social networking to give it life and content.

Why Should Leaders in Transformation Engage in Social Media?   The social media properties on the Web are exploding and are fast becoming a necessary part of the arsenal of any organization. It took 38 years for the radio to attract 50 million listeners, 13 years for television to gain the attention of 50 million viewers. The Internet took only four years to attract 50 million participants, and Facebook reached 50 million participants in only one and a half years. Launched in 2004 and originally designed for Harvard students and then expanded to the public, Facebook is a phenomenal example of social engagement gone wild. By 2009, Facebook achieved 100 million monthly active users covering all age groups ranging from 13 to 65 years. In 2011, there are approximately 500 million Facebook users.

This technology reflects our social behavior and is unlike any other. Many technologies are usually going against what we normally do. Technology adoption cycles have long been a function of the adaptability of the users. Social media and particularly networking is what is happening already except at a local scale. This gives one voice electronic power and scale. Historically, technology is injected into our business and society and requires a shift in our business practices and process or our culture. As social beings, social networking and media are something we do already.

Social Media Momentum Can Be Dangerous to Business   Consumers now expect companies to have a social media presence. Just like the radio, television, and the Internet drove advertising dollars, we expect social media to be monetized in some way. But how does an organization know how to get involved, participate, lead, or stay out? How do organizations measure and monetize this new approach to engaging customers, partners, and employees? What does success look like?

Answering these questions requires much more than quick responses. However, using a few good experiences may help frame these questions so that we can gain insight into this approach. Here are some sugg.estions:

- Don't look at social media only as an add-on to your current media offerings.
- Understand what others are doing with social media and compare your strategy to theirs.

Often, businesses want to know how they can get into social media. "I want to be in social media; how do I get in?" is not the best way to address this new approach. They get themselves a Facebook or Twitter identity; they get into social network technology and find their way into the blogosphere. They add these features to their media arsenal and sit and wait. They fail to acknowledge that social media/networking is not just a media outreach program; it is a new platform just as the personal computer was not an extension of the mainframe. Like the telephone is not an extension of ground mail, like an airplane is not an extension to a car, these are platforms designed to change the way we communicate. The personal computer was not an extension of the mainframe but many thought it should never be in the workplace when it first came out. I remember when I sat in front of one at Intel in the early 1980s and all I could think about it was "wow, what can I do with this now?" By the way, it was the size of the entire table and laptops were not even in our vernacular. But it was smaller than the mainframe and would have processing power that many dreamed of. In the early 1980s, one small operating system named Windows from a small company named Microsoft began to take hold. But the future was not defined. Document systems like Wang dominated the market, and Apple was just starting to challenge the sensibilities of the power users. It was going to change the manner of our interactions. So is social media. Like hardware and systems platforms, the social media platform resides in all these devices and yet is a virtual, connected but separate mode and media of connecting, engaging, and monetizing business. This requires us to view it differently, measure it differently, and monetize it differently.

What are others doing with social media? Organizations are experimenting in the following ways:

- Co-creating with new product designs with customers and prospects.
- Listening to the market and monitoring customer impressions.
- Connecting all vendors and partners in their value chain and being in constant dialog.
- Engaging customers using the networking as another advertising, messaging platform.
- Serving customers through the media.

To do these things, one must have a strategic view of social media and a tactical implementation capability, not a tactical adjustment to the budget. This media addition is not incremental add-ons but transformational (i.e., your teams must think and do differently). Second, social media teams must go where the customers meet and they must converse and connect. Business to business organizations find this difficult because they are not retail but wholesale in their approaches and all the systems in the organizations do not lend themselves to such retail one-to-one dialog. Furthermore, organizations are used to telling and talking than listening. In social media, people are talking, so listen more and talk less because the audience is very raw to insincerity. Authenticity is the calling card of any social networking exercise. You may think you are being heard, but you are ignored if you are self-serving. Next ambiguity and trust of the brand in the hands of your community of customers and prospects is not comfortable. Brand managers will state that the brand is about customer action, but when they see social media dialog and customers talking and acting over the brand of your company, it is not business as usual. Trusting the wisdom of crowds and acknowledging that one voice could destroy your brand is key in these endeavors. As organizations transform to be transparent, open to comment and also accepting of the ignorance of the masses in some cases, they mature to realize that their brand is an active agent of the social space. They realize that the better way to build a business is "with" customers talking on the Web, not "to" customers one-on-one in a controlled space.

Organizations should manage their entry into the social media space before measurement sets in. If we measure it too soon, it does not monetize. It is very similar to trying to monetize customer conversations or leads and prospects in a user group meeting. These statements are not designed to dodge the very important questions about money making and value. If we view this entry as a new competency and platform for dialog and then sales, we realize that measuring the amount of sales before platform creation is premature.

The Health-Care Industry: An Example of Transformation Accelerated by Social Media

People go to the Internet for health information about as much as their doctor. Research conducted by Regence, the Blue Cross Blue Shield affiliate in the Pacific Northwest, showed that 15 percent of survey participants trust the Internet more than their doctor. The fact that people are searching for health information more than any other form of information on the Internet tells us that the industry is changing. Participants go to social media to:

- See what other consumers say about health issues, medications, and treatments.
- Research on other consumers' views and experiences and knowledge as well as to post their views.
- Learn skills or get educated on a condition they wish to manage or manage for others.
- Get and give emotional support.
- Build awareness around a disease

Social networking technology harnesses the collective knowledge, ignorance, biases, and insights of the active participants. Cynics argue that much of these insights are incorrect and not based on evidence. This can be somewhat true, but the collective intelligence of crowds is what we live with every day. At parties, in every phone conference, and in every classroom, opinions on information are formed the same way. We think of analytics, but we function on collective impression even in medicine.

The Side Effect Could Be the Main Effect   There is ample evidence that social interactions improve health. In 1979, a large-scale California study showed that people with the lowest levels of social contact had mortality rates two to four and a half times greater than those with strong social networks. The Framingham Heart Study assessed the interconnected social network of 12,067 people reviewed over a decade. Research showed that social networks play a role in the spread of obesity.[23] Further studies based on the Framingham Heart Study have uncovered that social networks can be carriers of weight gain through friends, siblings, and others. The details of these findings are varied and cannot be generalized, but it does confirm the power of social networks, unaided by technology, measured over 32 years. This side effect could be the power of crowds in passing on good as well as not so good behaviors and impressions. This fundamental finding that networks spread biologic and behavior traits and even feelings tell us that we cannot walk into this lightly and must consider the side effects of our interactions and interventions.

The Four Ds of Social Media in Healthcare   Health care in the use of the Internet falls into four categories:

1. *Dialog—people talking to people.* It used to be that when a patient met with a physician, it was a one-way communication or symptom and resolution. Now, the patient is armed with information, research, questions, and also conversations with others who share the same symptoms. The patient brings his or her network of connected conversations to the doctor's office and might even rate the experience after. Or he or she may tweet about the event and share learnings. I call this "patient plus" because they bring their entire network of knowledge, relationships, and support with them.

   Even though there are very strong laws that protect patients from the misuse of medical and personal information, some patients are eager to share their profile and information on the Web either anonymously or not to help themselves or others. This unique phenomenon has been characterized as a movement from a "need to know" to a "need to share" culture by Forrester Research.[24]

   Pew research showed that 83 percent of people search online for health information and 57 percent are eager to share their new health or medical information. Furthermore, half of all online health information searches are on behalf of others and not the one who searches.[25]

   Dialog systems are proliferating as more and more consumers want relevant and timely understanding of medical and health information both directly and from others who share their needs.

   We are moving from a one-to-one environment to a many-to-many health information exchange.

2. *Diagnosis—people trying to find out what and why.* Patients give up private diagnosis to gain valuable treatment information and insights on the social media platforms and online communities. Of course, this is not encouraged, but it happens daily. Patients work on the Web to find information about their illness and converse with others about the complexity of their predicament.

   Physicians fact-check and problem-solve and also learn from one another using the social media platforms (e.g., www.sermo.com, where several hundred thousand U.S. physicians engage). As the social media platforms are now energizing a latent need to engage communities to collaborate for solutions, new business models and new products are emerging.

3. *Decisions—people trying to make a judgment on information and action.* No doubt that more and more information, correct and incorrect, is finding its way to the social platforms. In the past, medical information and conversations were private and paternalistic (i.e., top-down). Now the systems have democratized information giving it raw to all who wish to engage. Consumers want to make better decisions and are seeking to be consumers of health care, not patients of health care. As more and more information and dialog occur, consumers will look to these platforms to formulate decisions about treatments and costs. Most health-care sites have treatment-cost estimators and the like. At Regence, this feature is visited about 900 times a day and questions are asked of it as consumers make decisions about their treatments. Furthermore, consumers are shopping for doctors online and uncovering whom they want to be treated by. Consequently, 12,000 physicians have posted their profiles and approach on myRegence. com to differentiate their approaches.

4. *Delivery—people giving something to other people or organizations giving something to someone.* Many retailers like Dell and Best Buy have mastered selling on the Web, but they are also mastering social media to deliver value and gain insight. Hospitals and insurers are moving to deliver value through social media as well. In a sense, consumerism, health care, and retail are markets that are colliding in the next decade.

A number of hospitals are on Facebook, Twitter, and even YouTube, but it is still a small number compared to the 5,000-plus hospitals in the United States who are engaging in retail delivery. But times are changing and the digital health economy is slowly awakening. Health plans are also engaging and will have to accelerate their involvement as more and more individuals enter the system seeking advice and knowledge from others. As more consumers enter the health-care marketplace and demand the same experiences they receive in consumer and retail markets such as transparency, many-to-many conversations, greater understandings in real-time, and feedback, the systems will have to transform using social media.

Understanding the Value of Social Media and Social Networking Social media is more than media. It is a movement in which consumers and businesses engage in unstructured dialog, diagnosis, deliver, and decisions to purchase. Its language is conversational. It is commerce, where people purchase and community, where people gather, connect, and communicate.

It is a complex marriage of human sociology and technology that cannot be underestimated in its impact to the brand of an organization especially in markets that are transforming.

The choice as to when to engage, how to manage and measure, and whether to lead or to follow is not simple, but not impossible. These questions cannot be answered in general terms because the context and the market dynamics are strong variables in these decisions. We are all experimenting and learning. But some are courageous and have shown initial success, while others are cautious and may be holding their powder dry until they see bigger markets open.

Social networking and media are used by employees in their lives outside work. If your organization can engage people both at work and at home with their families in a cause greater than them, the possibilities of producing great outcomes at work are higher.

All in all, social media is about strategy and tactics not just tactics. It is a strategic instrument that transforms the organization that engages as much as it transforms the engagement with customers, employees, and partners. This is what strategy is made for. The challenge is to make the decisions when the unknowns of the market prevail. It is here where the great companies become greater as they make and serve markets and not respond to markets others have created.

Summary and Observations

While capability is about what you can do, competence is about the recipe of your capabilities and what you can do better than others consistently as far as your customers perceive.

First-order competencies are the set of skills and capabilities within the company that, if organized well, provide a strong, competitive advantage in the marketplace. Second-order competency is an overriding personality that an organization portrays to its customers and within. Consider the discussion about Sony and how whatever it does, it seems to make things smaller.

A recipe is what great organizations strive for. In transformational climates, linear approaches to capability are short-lived. If you believe that being good at one key capability is sufficient, you best make sure that it is nonreplicable.

Innovation, partnerships, and social media are key competencies of markets in transformation. When we cannot see or predict the future, we must imagine the possibilities and take calculated risks to define and enable that future. Innovation is based on ambiguity rather than predictability. This competence is not a corporate skill but a collective skill of teams and individuals who lend their creativity to the corporation. It is not one that can be turned into a competency easily because it is seldom linear, and not all ideas can be turned into big businesses. It is a competence that is more recipe than ingredient in that different people with the same elements of an idea could produce different results.

In transformation, organizations quickly realize that they can acquire others to build their teams, or they realize that they can align with others to sure up their capabilities to weather the storms ahead. Besides technology, three other competencies are essential for transforming your organization: partnerships, innovation, and social media.

Notes

1   Sony company profile. www.sony-europe.com/article/id/ 1178278971157.
2   C. K. Prahalad and Gary Hamel, "The Core Competence of the Corporation," *Harvard Business Review*, May–June 1990.
3   Ibid.
4   Michael Treacy and Fred Wiersema, *The Discipline of Market Leaders: Choose Your Customers, Narrow Your Focus, Dominate Your Market* (Boston: Addison-Wesley, 1997).
5   Meghan Meehan, "Forrester Features USAA as Social Media Innovator," May 13, 2010, www.bazaarvoice.com/blog/2010/05/13/forrester-features-usaa-as-social-media-innovator.

6   Steven Johnson, *Where Good Ideas Come From: The Natural History of Innovation* (New York: Riverhead Books, 2010).

7   Francis X. Frei, "Breaking the Trade-off between Efficiency and Service," *Harvard Business Review,* November 1, 2006, p. 97.

8   Noel M. Tichy, *The Leadership Engine: Building Leaders at Every Level* (New York: HarperCollins, 2007), p. 17.

9   Johnson, *Where Good Ideas Come From,* p. 193.

10   Johnson, *Where Good Ideas Come From,* p. 14.

11   Johnson, *Where Good Ideas Come From,* p. 45.

12   Johnson, *Where Good Ideas Come From,* p. 58.

13   Johnson, *Where Good Ideas Come From,* p. 61. This is explained through Kevin Dunbar, a psychologist at McGill University in the 1990s, who researched this.

14   Tom Kelley with Jonathan Littman, *The Art of Innovation: Lessons in Creativity from IDEO, America's Leading Design Firm* (New York: Currency, 2001), p. 107.

15   Kelley with Littman, *The Art of Innovation,* pp. 108–109.

16   "Top 10 slogans of the century." *Ad Age.* http://adage.com/century/slogans.html.

17   Tichy, *The Leadership Engine,* p. 16.

18   Vijay Govindarajan and Chris Trimble, *The Other Side of Innovation: Solving the Execution Challenge* (Boston: Harvard Business Press, 2010), pp. 13–14.

19   Ibid, p.12.

20   Clayton M. Christensen, *The Innovator's Dilemma: The Revolutionary Book that Will Change the Way You Do Business,* (New York: HarperCollins, 2003), p. 48.

21   Christensen, *The Innovator's Dilemma,* p. 182.

22   Frank posted in July 2010 that he was leaving Comcast. www.businessweek.com/managing/content/jan2009/ca20090113_373506.htm.

23   www.framinghamheartstudy.org/about/milestones.html.

24   Rob Koplowitz, Forrester Research, "Harnessing Social Networking to Drive Transformation," November 19, 2009, www.forrester.com/rb/Research/harnessing_social_networking_to_drive_transformation/q/id/55143/t/2.

25   Susannah Fox and Sydney Jones, "The Social Life of Health Information," *Pew Internet,* June 11, 2009, www.pewinternet.org/Reports/2009/8-The-Social-Life-of-Health-Information.aspx.

C H A P T E R

9

Sin #7: Expecting Flawless Execution without a Performance Platform

Organizations formulate their expectations with little idea as to whether they have the capacity or the talent to achieve the objectives. They tend to arrive at the conclusions only after they set the targets, goals, and measures. But as we plan for transformation, it is critical to find the talent ahead of time; find the capabilities of the future ahead of time; and to ensure that your operating capability anticipates rather than responds to a transformed market.

What if Starbucks could not handle the load of customer attention? The customers would leave and seldom return. What if Amazon. com could not ship products on time and accurately? The customers would go to the competition. So markets are seldom patient with mistakes in effective delivery of value because they have and make choices daily. And for every company that fails to satisfy a market need, one is waiting to take share away from them.

Execution is paramount to all executives but seldom is it asked if we have the platform set for such execution. A performance platform is an intentional construct that a corporation puts together that identifies its unique competency to deliver value to customers predictably and consistently. Starbucks delivers coffee the same way in the same taste to the same customer every time the customer demands it. This requires a performance platform. Corporations run to measurement as a way to monitor and change the ability to perform. As the sayings go, you measure what you manage, or if golf did not have a score, no one would play. These are fun sayings but they are not the same as saying that you would be a bad golfer if you did not measure yourself. There are many other reasons why you could be a bad golfer. One is that you may not have practiced; another is that you may have bad equipment; you may have poor eyesight or a host of other causes for the bad performance. Hence, it does not compute that measurement makes effectiveness in business. It computes that effective companies measure their performance of value to their customers.

Reconsidering your golf game, if you have a performance platform that converges all the elements of your performance, then maybe you could play well. This could range from exercise, eating, mental fitness, practice, a good coach, and time. In an organization, it would have similar traits but we can break them up into the classic areas of process, people, and technology. Corporations that succeed in managing their performance work at four dimensions of performance.

Two Elements of a Performance Platform

The following are the two categories of performance management:

1. *Human performance management.* This category is about inspiring, organizing work, people performance, and incentives.
2. *Corporate performance management.* This is about analytics, tools, systems, and methods around the financial, operational, customer, and strategic outcomes and outputs of a corporation.

Even though people are the basic asset in human performance, we will focus on the corporate performance platform tools in this section.

Four Dimensions of Corporate Performance Management

Corporations want to measure things that matter to them. Hence, to claim that any one methodology enables better measurement of the right things seems ludicrous and somewhat condescending. Many ways work for many people. However, measurement is one aspect of a performance platform that gets most of the attention and action. Organizations run to measurement as a security over execution problems. There are four elements to a performance platform that bring execution:

1. *Monitoring.* The art and science of observing and coaching employee activities and work.
2. *Measurement.* The art and science of gauging, using numbers and metrics and targets, how we are performing the tasks.
3. *Management.* The art and science of motivating, coaching, and enabling individuals and teams in the achievement of an objective.
4. *Direction setting.* The art and science of discovering strategic and tactical directions that are unique and differentiating in the marketplace, communicating this to all levels in the organization in the form that they can identify, and co-relating their day-to-day actions to goals.

Transformative markets demand acute capabilities in these four tactical aspects of performance. In order to perform at these four levels, successful corporations create a performance platform. Otherwise, flawless execution cannot be achieved except as a fluke of performance. There are three subsystems that make up a performance platform to achieve the above four elements of performance.

Understanding the biases of an organization involves three separate emphases points of view. They are the people, technology, and process subsystems:

1. People-focused
2. Process-focused
3. Technology-focused

Mistakes can be made in the early phases of a transformation exercise by introducing new technologies to a primarily process-driven organization. Conversely, transformation champions who talk about people issues to a primarily technology-focused organization may not succeed. Simply, understanding your organization's bias and viewpoint will guide you into introducing the ideas and technology of transformation. More often than not, transformation champions are very focused on introducing the concepts of transformation to their peers and management. Many can do better to understand the way and through which lens their peers and management view their world. Let's explore some stereotypical perspectives for all three views.

People-focused subsystems tend to:

- View their world through human issues.
- Believe that if people are motivated and happy, all is well.
- Believe that profits are important but people must be content for profits to be achieved.
- Believe that layoffs are traumatic and not an option.
- Believe that firings are contemplated for a long time.
- Train their people and develop them.
- Permit human resources and management to guide the company.
- Believe that communication is key.

Process-focused subsystems are:

- Really excited about organized initiatives.
- Get things done by project management.
- View the world through optimizing rather than removing processes.
- View the world through finite processes, activities, and tasks.
- Value you if you are a member of a process.
- Tend to have operating teams rule.
- Process life-cycles drive product life cycles

Technology-driven subsystems are:

- Bits-and-bytes oriented.
- The first to upgrade systems.
- Information technology-focused and motivated.
- Enjoy the latest and greatest technological development.
- Are early adopters of new technology.
- Very change driven and sometimes forget about evolutionary change and compatibilities.

Naturally, organizations can display any one of these subsystems at different times and they can also display various tendencies within large organizations. Every organization has an underlying harmonic

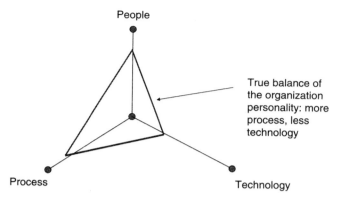

People

True balance of
the organization
personality: more
process, less
technology

Process   Technology

Exhibit 9.1   Signature of Your Organization

of a personality, which is probably not aligned to one subsystem or the other but somewhere in between. Exhibit 9.1 can assist in the understanding of the organizational center of gravity.

Let's assume that you have drawn these biases to that shown in the exhibit. Essentially, your organization deals with issues with the following priority:

1. People
2. Process
3. Technology

Taking a strong look at your transformation objectives, and the ways in which to approach (or have approached) a project, outline the personality and center of gravity of the transformation program. The center of gravity is the unique balance of the above three priorities within the organization. If the transformation objectives are not aligned, then the program is creating a paradox in introducing the goals and objectives with the natural biases of the audience. Exhibit 9.2 shows such a paradox.

Educating the Enterprise about Transformation with an Eye to the Dominant Subsystem

Those who have a plan to educate their teams and organizations tend to create and reinforce the need for transformation as a business imperative rather than a "nice to-do." Transformation champions

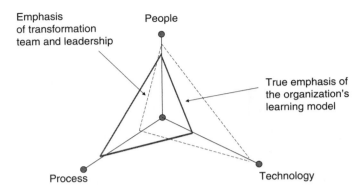

Exhibit 9.2   Paradox in Implementing Transformation

learn about transformation through books, conferences, and user groups among other ways. Their learning is usually rapid while the learning of their organization is much slower. A transformation program success can be corelated with the level of learning and commitment of the organization as a whole. For transformation to fully deploy knowledge to be top of mind of operating teams and for them to make good decisions with this information, teams all around the organization must learn about what transformation entails and its value to the future.

Learning can be accelerated by slowing the process into three steps with an eye to the dominant subsystem that your organization functions with:

1. *Education*—tell me what it is
2. *Pilot*—let me try it
3. *Enterprise*—let me deploy it fully

Programs move from one phase to the next in sequence (see Exhibit 9.3). Individuals, teams, and organizations also take the similar learning path. In a transformation program, several forces resist this learning:

- The inertia of the way things are
- The inertia of fearing the unknown; what is known is safer
- The inertia of learning without tools and focus
- The inertia of too much to do

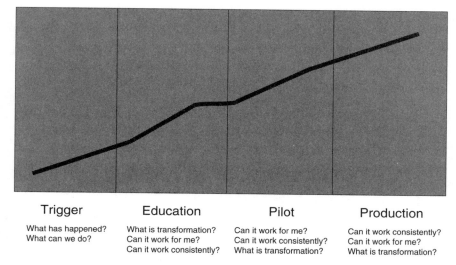

Trigger	Education	Pilot	Production
What has happened? What can we do?	What is transformation? Can it work for me? Can it work consistently?	Can it work for me? Can it work consistently? What is transformation?	Can it work consistently? Can it work for me? What is transformation?

Exhibit 9.3   Phases of Transformation Implementation

- The inertia of being measured on other performance measures
- The inertia of fearing loss of job security

The seminal work of Peter Senge in his book *The Fifth Discipline* has focused us onto the art and science of collective organizational learning. Transformation programs start, grow, and die with "learning disabilities"[1] as their poison. Does your organization have any learning techniques that have worked in the past? How does your organization learn new ideas and implement them? Does your organization have blind spots (i.e., do they not notice people issues)?

Understanding the Organizational Dominant Subsystem Demands Observations

Every organization has dominant subsystems—they tend to emphasize people, process, or technology in their tactics. Stephen Covey,[2] one of the more popular thought leaders and authors of our time, has often been quoted as asking us to seek to understand before being understood.

Ultimately, the failure of the transformational educational process is seldom a failure of the team or organization. It is usually a failure of mismatching of the educational tools and techniques with the methods of learning and communicating within an organization (i.e., the emphasized subsystem). Each subsystem learns differently and must be acknowledged in the way they learn about transformation. If I were communicating to an engineering subsystem, I would concentrate my examples around the technological changes that drive transformation and how the business needs this to be implemented well. Of course, one can force this learning by getting the person in the corner office to dictate the need and the methods of technology and methodology absorption. One can get very far with this but all that results is a short-term high-amplitude event. CEOs seldom have bandwidth to keep the attention and the loud voice on this topic indefinitely. Hence, transformation champions understand that to really transform the organization, you need a programmatic approach combined with a sense that to change others we must first model and change ourselves.

If each subsystem learns differently and no one organization is people, process, or technology but a mix, how do we help them frame a massive transformation in the marketplace after we have a held all the meetings and the web communications on the intranet and the CEO speeches? What are the things to watch out for in the day-to-day functions and what philosophies do we hold dear in our movement toward transformation when we are working on the performance platform to execute our cause?

People Subsystem

The people dimension of a performance platform that is preparing for transformation is based on action steps that propel transformation in individuals and teams in your organization.

Action Step #1: Learning the Art of Failing Successfully

Failure is never good? Not really. We learn in school that failure is learning. We learn that you can never become better until you come back from failure. We enjoy watching that in movies, the theater, and we always clap when we see the failure turn to success. But when we enter the business world, failure seems career limiting. So how do we transform the business the first time out and ourselves? It may be possible but not practical. The lessons in failure are that big mistakes are made by a compounded set of decisions because one decision seldom kills a thriving organization. So there is so much hope to turn a bad decision into a set of decisions that succeed but we can't see the bad decision among the good.

Action Step #2: Starting and Then Changing with Market Expectation

"Failing forward" is a term I use to identify a behavior that successful transformational companies have as a platform for execution. These companies move forward with mistakes and power their way to ulti-mate success. Honda did this in its initial releases. Hyundai had initial problems prior to its current successes. Vinay Couto, Frank Ribeiro, and Andrew Tipping speak of it as sense and adjust to describe the way in which companies sensitive to transformation in markets release products, test them, and adjust them as they learn and grow to become very strong companies that listen to the unknown unknowns in the markets they serve.

> To navigate such a rocky landscape, companies must be ready to repeatedly transform themselves—indeed, to institutionalize the capacity to alter strategies again and again—as business conditions require.[3]

Action Step #3: Nurturing Cultures of Nonconformance

CEOs like to have people who respect them. They translate respect into obedience. I have witnessed many a tabletop argument where an employee challenged the ideas of the senior leadership. The fires will burn and the thunderbolts fly and the CEO and management team hold their ground till the words die down and there is silent perceived agreement. Weeks later, the leadership actually changes their minds but never acknowledges that it was challenge that made that happen.

There is a fine line between a challenging team and insubordi-nate behaviors. The transformational teams who value flawless execution build a platform of appropriate questioning. We make the mistake of removing every challenging sound assuming that quiet resistance will leave as well. Failing organizations believe that con-formance within the "rules" symbolize motion. They believe that motion is smooth without challenging spots. But true execution momentum is driven by other more nonlinear, subtle forces.

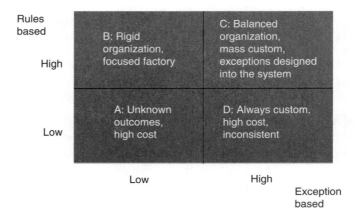

Exhibit 9.4   Execution Balance

Leaders focused on execution evangelize and are culture filters. They draw out the inner vision of the organization and filter the culture away from naysayers and retain the challengers who actually question the directions and the techniques.

Exhibit 9.4 identifies the careful balance between conforming execution teams and challenging teams and those that are uniform in style and diverse in style. Removing all diverse ideas and challenging ideas can create a highly aligned organization or a revolt depending on how you manage the business. We will explore more of this balance in this chapter when we explore the Process subsystems.

Action Step #4: Balancing Business Performance and Culture

In this rapidly changing business climate, a CEO must perform or perish. "A CEO is always on a 90-day employment contract," says the CEO of a large high-tech company. You slip and you fall forever. Given the financial debacles compounding the issues, CEOs are not trusted until they prove themselves. The natural consequences of realizing the lonely CEO role can be isolation and focus on the financial results as the end, not the means. After all, no CEO gets fired for high performance with unhappy people in these challenging times. So why worry about culture when change is about to happen and transformation is ahead? Just drive for success and culture will follow, right? Everyone talks of culture, but a high performance culture that produces is more important—is it not?

The inadequacy with this model is twofold. First, it really does not work in the short term to be inhumane and get performance. It will take tremendous energy to recycle employees, work the politics that emerges due to your politics, and to ensure that you don't get fired in the process. The attention of the organization goes away from the work and to protecting their jobs at a time where focus on work and risking your job will allow for transformation to be successful. In transformational times, organizations should focus on the building of a new culture that can withstand dramatic shifts and then exit the transformation in a leading position. The same energy focused and applied to the cultural development of an organization results in regular, predictable reactions that permit a CEO to focus on other growth-oriented strategies. If the goal of a CEO is to be surgical and not be a blunt knife, he should spend time developing a culture of competence, not be a guardian of guilt and fear. No one can innovate in fear and scarcity (i.e., what I got, you want to take away). It is in an environment of opportunity and perceived but controlled abundance that risks are taken.

Abundance does not mean you get what you want. It means that we build, act, and invest in the future and we take the educated risks where appropriate. We don't send everyone to his or her cubicles and tell them times are bad, so get out and make "it" happen. When they do not even have confidence that "it" can happen in the environment created, telling them to pull their socks up and get it done is meaningless rhetoric. Today, 90-day probations are a way of life in business. Why let that stop us from creating 2,000-day programs that live beyond our own existence while we are executing on current-day activities that frame our present?

So during a crisis of transformation, do we focus on long-term cultural transformation as a performance platform or do we get on with current-day performance demands and let the culture follow? Or do we do something nebulous like balance both priorities?

Many will say that we should do something in between or depends on the situation. These are appropriate answers but challenging to implement. The power of recognizing that culture transformation is the basis of business transformation is that culture is a necessary ingredient to creating a strong business outcome. But we don't have to work on one then the other. We work on both because we must deal with today's tools and work on building our new tools for tomorrow. Culture is the output measure that never ends in the quest for a stronger performance platform. But business results are the outcome measures of the decisions we make daily played upon by people living in the culture you build.

Action Step #5: Establishing Bullets and Toilet Paper

In wartime, soldiers need the basics before they will reach for high performance. Whimsical though it seems, I call this "bullets and toilet paper." It illustrates the value of logistics and backup talent placed behind any powerful front-facing team. Bullets signify the ammunition and training an organization gives the front-facing forces while toilet paper signifies the valuable back-end logistics. Early in my life, I was an infantry soldier. In the course of this training, I learned that there is more value for me to stay with my battalion than run ahead. Making it first to battle without my team meant only that I died. Bullets and toilet paper keep the teams running together because individualism has little place in battle. You just get killed first.

Care and feeding of any team is important but in building a performance-centered execution platform, a leader should understand the subtlety of too much transparency and too little transparency. Once, I witnessed a team-building exercise with sales and marketing and engineering teams in which the vice president of engineering spent 20 minutes informing everyone of the problems he had with his team and how the product was limited in quality without talking about what he could do to make it succeed. He probably believed in being transparent. However, this level of transparency showed his limits and more than that, it showed that now the sales teams knew that anything could go wrong. Driving back to the analogy of bullets and toilet paper, it would be okay to say that the bullets jam in the rifle *x out of x times* and finish with that. Then talk about how to deal with that situation. It's not ok to just be transparently incompetent. Executives who are chartered to provide bullets and toilet paper are custodians of business and team confidence and cannot relinquish that responsibility by merely being transparent. Fundamentally, a performance platform is about getting the basics done very well. Then, building from that, redefining an experience with customers.

Technology Subsystem

The technology subsystems of a performance platform should not be considered just computers and software. Rather, it is about how technology is viewed (i.e., as a platform or a series of technologies combined to serve a purpose). It is about the way we view technology not as bits and bytes but as a performance platform for the future.

Action Step #1: Chasing Technology Trajectories for Optimization

Technology can make business productive. But technology alone cannot do this without process and people transformation. A poorly managed business process with the incorrect outputs or outcomes if placed on a more efficient system can only deliver incorrect outcomes faster. In the domain of technology, inertia also sets in. I have said often that God created the earth in six days and rested on the seventh day because he did not have an installed base! New technologies seldom bring immediate purchases especially when there is an installed base of customers who like what you have built. Early adopters will pick some up but only to try. It takes time and adoption curves to build a real legacy of transformation. Customers seldom change until key forces compel them to do so. Successful transformational leaders know that technology can accelerate change. They know that they must be on that curve but to bank on that adoption curve and jump around looking for the next big untested thing is not effective. Disruptive technologies exist in any industry and any CEO must protect the company from the disruption. But one tends to assume that disruptive means advanced and untested technology. Many of the more disruptive technologies are those that just solve important problems those customers encounter in simple, elegant, and low-cost ways. More and more, disruption is coming in the form of low-cost, highly potent solutions from the East, where they served the masses rather than early adopters. This is called "reverse innovation" in certain circles as the solutions are tested for the masses who cannot afford innovation as it is currently priced.

Action Step #2: Transformative Technology or Platform?

The iPad seems like a cool product because people buy it for the applications. But it is strategically placed as a platform for innovation with applications of all kinds that redefine the use of the iPad. The value of such a platform is that the platform can be a chassis, like the car you drive with the applications being options you purchase. The iPad has also captured the imagination of the corporations putting the device into various uses.[4] This chassis can be your performance platform. As you see applications you want, you can add them to your chassis. If you want an application, don't purchase a chassis just because you might want it someday. Organizations do exactly that with no regard to the consequences. That would be like purchasing a car for the navigation system. Transformational organizations must decide how they configure their technology infrastructure and identify the platforms they are deploying from the applications they are using. This configuration will power the businesses they are targeting and should give these strategies lift. What usually happens is that technology becomes another strategy rather than empowering strategy. Technology becomes another strategy when it becomes disjointed from the business itself and becomes something that the business must contend with to achieve their objectives.

Process Subsystem

There are four classifications to business operating capability:

1. An organization that functions on rules
2. An organization that functions without rules
3. An organization that functions with no flexibility to exceptions
4. An organization that functions with flexibility to exceptions

Everyone can declare that they want to be an agile organization that can seek and respond while keeping to the set of objectives. But how can you be flexible yet rigid?

Exhibit 9.4 is a chart of this dilemmas placed in quadrants. One may argue that an organization that functions with rules makes no exceptions. So why have quadrants? Well, this is the dilemma that we are to explore.

Quadrant A symbolized a chaotic environment with no rules and no exceptions. Obviously, this will cost as a platform for performance. Quadrant B symbolizes a rigid rule-based organization where no exceptions are allowed. A focused factory doing repeated activities with tight quality standards may fit this expectation. Quadrant D is where every request is an exception, and the costs will skyrocket while every customer will have a custom solution. Quadrant C is the appropriate environment for a transformative performance platform. The Toyota performance system has both the rigid characteristics as well as the ability to flex on demand. It has mastered the art of "efficient agility." In their 1999 article on the system, Steven Spear and H. Kent Bowen declare that it is its very rigidity that makes them flexible when they break the activities down to key units that connect to each other and gain agile response to feedback.[5] This system and platforms like this allow for extreme operational focus while exceptions are designed into the system.

The challenge with building a platform for transformation is founded in the difficulty of designing an operational platform built on deterministic outcomes for a strategy that is preparing for non-deterministic outcomes.

Basics of Business Intelligence

There are three elements of learning in a transformed organization about where it must go:

1. *Eyesight*—the ability of an organization to see ahead and scan the arena of transformation.
2. *Foresight*—the ability of an organization to understand where and what the future will bring or hold.
3. *Insight*—the ability of an organization to find the core-differentiating variable that define the markets of the future and see the noise in the market that distorts understanding from the signals that the market is sending during transformation.

Tools provide eyesight and maybe some foresight, but insight comes from people. Even though this book concentrates on the tools, the basis for business intelligence is people who can be business intelligent—people, who have the knowledge and wisdom to collect, correlate, and understand cause and effect of markets. Let us run through some tools that may assist in creating a toolset for eyesight and foresight in your performance platform:

- Business process engineering
- Activity-based costing
- Business intelligence and information analytics
- Supply-chain management
- Balanced scorecard
- Lean and six sigma

Business Process Engineering

Michael Hammer and James Champy, the fathers of Reengineering, defined business process reengineering as:

> . . . fundamental rethinking and radical re-design of business processes to achieve dramatic improvements in critical, contemporary measures of performance, such as cost, quality, service, and speed.[6]

They outlined the following key words in this definition:

- Fundamental
- Radical
- Dramatic
- Processes

The world embraced this approach and took to it by storm. Today, many believe that more than 50 percent of these initiatives have not lived up to their claim. As early as 1994, American companies spent $32 billion on business reengineering and two-thirds failed. Yet, let's examine the reengineering promise. Their promise was that dramatic results could be achieved by redesigning processes using contemporary performance measure. But many just redesigned processes to improve speed rather than look at what to improve first using all contemporary measures available. A key contemporary measure of cost is activity-based cost management (ABC/M). With it, one can focus on areas of improvement rather than speed up efficiently that which is non-value-added in the first place. In many ways, ABC should be performed before any other initiative is engaged so that organizations can learn where to target their initiatives.

Activity-Based Cost Management

Activity-based costing (ABC) was developed as a practical solution to managing overhead. In the 1980s, many companies, based on the findings[7] of Professor Robert Kaplan of Harvard Business School, Professor Robin Cooper, and Professor H. Thomas Johnson of Portland State University, began to realize that traditional accounting systems and cost management methodologies were distorting how overhead should be associated with the product and services the company performed. This is not due to incorrectness but because the nature of overhead had changed and transformed while the methods that treated overhead had not. Traditional systems did not evolve to support the changing behavior of costs. In the past, managers had to put up with this thing called "overhead" which was charged to their departments while they knew well that these costs were incorrectly allocated to them.

In the 1980s, the Consortium of Advanced Manufacturing-International (CAM-I) defined ABC as "a methodology that measures the costs and performance of activities, resources and cost objects."[8]

Spurred by the lead articles and books from enlightened thought leaders[9] and a great need in the field for an answer to where overhead is going, ABC began to be viewed as an initiative in the 1990s. Unfortunately, billed as a replacement for then current cost management methods, ABC began to take on the general ledger (GL). This did not work. Even though the industry has moved beyond this, stigma still exists in the minds of new entrants and curious, new discoverers of ABC in the field. They ask, "Does it replace the GL?"

Beginning in the manufacturing industry, ABC served a strong need for firms who were struggling to identify a means of:

- Measuring how products and services consume overhead.
- Understanding the true costs of activities within organizations.
- Understanding the true costs of products and services.
- Understanding the true profitability of channels, products, and services.
- Quantifying, measuring, analyzing, and improving business processes.

The early 1990s were filled with ABC endeavors that were billed as change initiatives that would reengineer the finance output. These initiatives moved from the pure manufacturing companies to cover the process manufacturing industry, the service industry, and the government. They were generated out of visionary finance teams and champions targeted as a cost cutting initiative. They were endorsed by chief financial officers who were challenged to improve the profitability death spirals of their corporations or in the case of government to do more with less and to justify budgets. Likened to liposuction, ABC would be used to identify dreaded overhead and assign this large and undefined beast into its correct cage. ABC served a strong purpose then since traditional cost methodologies tended to allocate costs directly to products and services with a single-stage allocation. Costs are allocated based on labor or standard overhead volume drivers. Labor hours, traditionally being the larger portion of total overhead mix, would drive the decision of where to put overhead costs.

A description of the evolution of ABC can be found in *Implementing Activity-based Cost Systems* by John Miller[10] and in *The Ernst & Young Guide to Total Cost Management* by Ostrenga, Ozan, McIhattan, and Harwood.[11] *Activity-based Information Systems: An Executive's Guide to Implementation* is also a resource.[12]

Business Intelligence and Information Analytics

There is no end to the number of systems vendors and consulting firms that are focused onto business intelligence and analytics. Some are oriented toward visualization tools while others are focused on the underlying infrastructure and data environment. These tools are rooted in the dream of making data into decisions. They are at the heart of the information revolution.

Christopher Meyer, author of *Fast Cycle Time* and *Blur*, emphasizes that:

> Marketing tracks market share, operations watches inventory, finance monitors costs and so on. Such results measures tell an organization where it stands in its effort to achieve goals but not how it got there or, even more important, what it should do differently.[13]

It is estimated that only 3 to 5 percent of corporate information is analyzed. Why is this not a surprise? Watch any business in the 2000s and note that executives are inundated with faxes, electronic mail, telephone messages, conference proceedings, direct mail, tele-marketing calls, paper mail, and reports. In fact, if they actually read and analyzed everything they received, they would not do anything productive to improve our organizations. Just when they thought they had control over information, the Internet will revolutionize information accessibility and is transforming the very way in which business is performed. Now executives find themselves surfing, for hours and hours, the Web, setting triggers and agents to trap information swimming by their keyboards.

Business is not getting any more manageable. With corporate intranets, extranets, knowledge network and social technologies entering the information management landscape in the Global 100, corporations will never die from starvation when it comes to information. They may die from indigestion. Too much and too fast, data with no analytical framework and no action seem to be the death slogan for the Global 100.

If your company is suffering from data obesity and knowledge starvation, the symptoms are the following:

- *Data disintegration.* Do you go to a limited number of sources for information or do you have to send out a search party?
- *Context insensitive information.* When you receive information, is it immediately applicable for performance measures you have set or does it require that you preprocess this information?
- *Fitness of sources.* Is information timely and credible?
- *Depth of information.* Does the information you receive force new questions?
- *Data dimensionality.* Does the information provide dimensional views and perspectives, that is, what if I wanted only those products and services to customer A and channel B?
- *Timeliness.* Do you find that your organization gives you information that is at least one quarter too late?
- *Data usefulness.* Have you tested the value of the information you put out by not sending it out to see the reaction?

Equally important, information is not always viewed as an asset in organizations. Recently, the push for more and more information is having some negative effects:

- The value of information diminishes with time. Old, untimely information can be extremely destructive to the natural flow of business. Assumptions are made with data and these assumptions could halt the successful momentum of a company's actions on products and services.
- Information may have negative value when it is not only untimely but also wrong. Wrong or outdated information may lead you to the wrong conclusions.
- The value of information is relationship dependent, that is, finite data is useless without the correct context and the relationship of the finite data to other finite data (e.g., knowing about costs overruns in your factory is relevant but more relevant when you can understand where and what caused them).

In a nutshell, information, when unused, updated, and unrelated, is a depreciating asset and can turn into a liability very quickly.

Self-Knowledge: The New Information Frontier   In the past, business enjoyed increasing market share and profits abounded. With the global competitiveness splitting the market pies, these companies are fast realizing that they must do more with what talent and tools they have.

In the search for the ultimate "magic pill," be it operational efficiency, gaining loyal customers, building a new mousetrap, or establishing a powerful value chain of vendors and suppliers, companies have discovered that the true lasting competitive advantage is not just the above-mentioned strategic themes but knowledge. Knowledge has long since been the theme song of the management gurus of the past century. But knowing without doing can be a waste of time and energy.

Beyond this discovery, the Global 100 is fast realizing that "self-knowledge" and applied self-knowledge is true power (i.e., knowing yourself better than your competitor knows you, to act on your strengths effectively in your market space). For example, Walmart changed the way manufacturers, brokers, retailers, and wholesalers performed work. Walmart changed the entire business model and activities in the food industry. Knowing what they did well and knowing what their competitors did not know about the consumer brought Walmart to victory with a 3 percent profit margin in the same businesses that its competitors enjoy a less than 1 percent margin.

Winning in the food industry, which is a $500 billion business, Walmart has triggered the industry into a cost-cutting efficiency adventure that will remove $30 billion in cost over the next five years to their competitors. Walmart used its self knowledge and applied it for customer retention. More than information technology, Walmart understands how to get the best from its technology, vendors, and customers better than some others do.

Data Is Doubling Every Two Years   Gordon Moore, cofounder of Intel Corporation, introduced the notion of complexity growth when he declared that the microprocessor would double in complexity every two years.[14] The prediction has borne out to be a fact since. It is believed that in the years to come, more power will exist in a single computer on your desk that is the equivalent of all the computer power combined in our world today. Similarly, it is believed conservatively, that the amount of private and corporate data stored on computers is doubling every 12 to 18 months. Clearly, it is not a lack of information that holds corporations back.

Neither is it information technology. Faye Borthick, professor of Accounting at Georgia State University and Harold Roth, professor of Accounting at the University of Tennessee in Knoxville, declare, "For the first time, information technology is sufficiently well developed that accountants can have the information they want."[15]

With the introduction of data warehousing, data marting, data mining, online analytical processing, three-tier client-server technologies, desktop navigation tools, search engines, cloud-based information management and hardware technologies, information technology seems to have popped up like intelligent mushrooms waiting to consume data and expel it to anyone at anytime and anywhere. These technologies coupled with the entire information overload will only bring irrelevant data to us faster. Winning companies don't win by mastering quick access to information; they master the ability to, at a sustainable level, provide relevant information to the right people at the right time for the right managerial decision.

Peter Drucker stated that what is important is not tools but the concepts behind them.[16] He declared that a conceptual map is sadly lacking in today's information to give it relevance to the decision maker. In some ways, the technological treadmill is going faster and faster almost outstripping the needs of business and creating a life of its own.[17] This new market demand for executives to be powered by information to win gives birth to the knowledge leader, one who drives his business using analytical information as guide. The knowledge leader must now understand the fundamental competitive capability using these newfound tools is not how much information is gathered but understand that the leader must optimize the mean time between decisions (MTBD). He must improve how fast he can turn data into decisions to create a new landscape for his competitors to chart or be lost in the maze of information.

Information Is No Longer Power   Today, the knowledge leader cannot be measured by what information is obtained and dispensed but by what information is rejected, which will be significantly more. Without keen selection capability, the knowledge leader will crush under the sheer weight and demand of decisions to be made. Vijay Govindarajan put it in the context of innovation:

> Ongoing operations are a world of 90 percent data, 10 percent unknowns. A bold innovative initiative, on the other hand, might be just the reverse with ten percent data and ninety percent unknowns. In such a situation, if all you can talk about is the data, then you are talking about only 10 percent of what matters.[18]

Consequently, organizations that master the abilities to understand enough to make decisions command themselves enough to act decisively and consistently will win. Information seems powerless. Decisive actions using relevant information are power. Competitive advantage is best developed in the acquisition and deployment of relevant information to all who need and decide/act with it. What used to be in the careful hands of business analysts will shift dramatically to all managers and decision makers. There is no longer time for hierarchical decision-making protocols. Only time for hierarchy to hold the old bones of the corporation in place while the nervous system of the company fights the real wars of wealth acquisition. Relevant data is the fuel for this activity.

What Brings Relevance to Information? [19]   Peter F. Drucker, the father of modern management, in his seminal article, "The Information Executives Truly Need," contends that information should challenge basic assumptions and have links to strategy.

Drucker states that enterprises are paid to create wealth not control costs. But this premise is not reflected in traditional measurements. First-year accounting students are taught that the "balance sheet portrays the liquidation value of the enterprise and provides creditors with worst case information. But enterprises are not normally run to be liquidated."[20]

Drucker seems to believe that information is used for wealth creation. He breaks up information value into four main value categories:

1. *Foundation information:* diagnostic, cash flow
2. *Productivity information:* resource productivity
3. *Competence information:* measurement of the unique ability that Customers pay for
4. *Resource-allocation information:* managing scarce resources for the current business

Note that he believes these to be information on the current business condition and hence tactical in nature. Simply put, many organizations today are running forward looking backward. These companies are blind to the strategic relationships among their true product value, their profitability, and their channel behavior. They lack the most basic of intelligence systems even to answer the more basic questions like "are your cycle time for your products and your cost of product creation co-related?" That is, do they track with one another? If so, what are the drivers of product demand and profit?

John Whitney, professor of Management at Columbia University and author of *Strategic Renewal for Business Units*, hit the nail on the head when he declared:

> Indeed, I have found that perhaps most businesses do not know the true accrual profit of their products and services, and fewer still know the profitability of customers.[21]

Supply-Chain Management

Supply-chain management (SCM) has moved to the forefront of business analytics and has captured the imagination of many organizations whose lifeblood flows in their logistics to and from the customer. SCM is the science and art of driving value through the value chain be it ensuring shoes get to market or groceries get through the broker-retailer-manufacturer chain rapidly and at least overhead costs.

Balanced Scorecard

As the title implies, balanced scorecard is a methodology to solve the following challenges with the execution of strategy. It:

- Provides a balance between certain relatively opposing forces in strategy:
  - Between internal and external influences
  - Between leading and lagging indicators and measures
  - Between financial and nonfinancial goals
  - Between organizational silos focused on their own goals and an overarching framework of goals
  - Between finance priorities and operations
- Aligns strategic goals with objectives, targets, and metrics
- Cascades to all levels of the organization

In a nutshell, this methodology, which makes strategy actionable, can be viewed as:

- A methodology to manage your business strategy
- A common language at all levels of your organization
- A common set of principles to manage the day-to-day as well as to framework your strategy
- A measurement system to identify and manage business purpose

Balanced scorecard is not about measurement; it is about translating strategy into action at all levels of the organization. But in its root is the principle of motivated action (i.e., granting the individuals and teams within the organization the ability to know that their actions feed a strategic focus every day).

A three-year study by the Chartered Institute of Personnel and Development (CIPD) was targeted at understanding how good management practices influence performance. Greater performance was found in 6 out of 12 sample companies, companies whose people are stimulated to do their jobs and serve customers. Furthermore, all six of the selected organizations used balanced scorecard or a comparative method.[22] Since then, countless organizations have deployed the balanced scorecard effectively.[23]

An Argument for Balance and Focus   It is often stated, in business, that focus is the key to achieving a goal. Hence, the natural efforts of senior management are to cut anything that does not fit the goal. Analogies like "being laser-like" or "putting the wood behind the arrow" speak to the ideas of singularity in goals and focus. Some of these analogies actually speak to the art of war and to battle strategies as comparatives. On a tactical level, on the ground sales and marketing battles do need this level of focus. But strategic focus is built on another set of analogies that are more applicable—not a single focus but a focus on a set of competencies applied upon a small set of strategic themes. The battle of strategy cannot be one of singular focus because the elements necessary to perform a strategy demand balance—a balance of activities within the organization to achieve the tactical wins.

British forces in Singapore during World War II focused all their defenses out to sea to guard against the Japanese forces they thought would attack from the South China Sea. The British were imbalanced in their strategic intent. The Japanese forces, however, walked into Singapore from the north via a three-quarter-mile causeway that connected the Malayan peninsula to Singapore and conquered the small but strategic port. The lack of a balanced view of the corporate theater, just like the battlefield theater, could cause similar results.

Battle strategies teach us that strategic and tactical wins must build momentum and also competencies for future battles. Today, battles are not won the way they were many years ago. Today, forces must win multiple battles at the same time in multiple theaters with a limited budget and resources. Exhibit 9.5 illustrates the key value of balance in balanced scorecards. The key factors of looking in and out for indicators assists organizations in building insight into scorecarding.

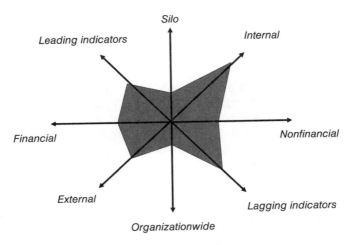

Exhibit 9.5   The Insight that Balance Brings to Scorecards

Balance between Internal and External Factors   Organizations that build competencies for tomorrow while winning the battles of today are responding to "balance." Organizations that understand, acknowledge, and exploit both the internal and the external factors in assessing their strategy understand balance. Many times, organizations focus only on the internal aspects of their business (i.e., the operational aspects of getting product to market) but not the challenges of selling and marketing or the condition of the market. Many times, this syndrome is called "build it and they will come."

Balance in Leading and Lagging Indicators   Peter Drucker, founder of modern management, states that "we need measurements for a company or industry that are akin to the 'leading indicators' and 'lagging indicators' that economists have developed during the past half-century to predict the direction in which the economy is likely to move and for how long."[24]

Similarly, financial measures found in balance sheets and income statements and other statutory reports are mainly lagging indicators to a business (i.e., they tell you what has occurred not what could). Most information in the news and in the magazines seems to be lagging indicators. Most of the information on past sales, production performance, and so on are lagging indicators of performance because they tell you where you have been and how you have performed. Leading indicators are signs of future performance or situations. For example, if you noticed that your daughter, who had a fever, was using a thermometer, that would be a lagging indicator of illness. But if you saw your daughter sneezing earlier or returning home sluggishly, that would be a leading indicator. The power of a balanced strategic performance system is to acknowledge both leading and lagging indicators which allows corporations to balance past results with future drivers of performance.

Balance between Financial and Nonfinancial Measures   Many corporate leaders tend to think in terms of numbers:

> Perhaps the most recognizable defect of financial-only goals is the barrier that inevitably blocks the translation of overall corporate financial goals into sub goals that people in the enterprise can pursue with confidence.[25]

They measure progress in financial terms and believe that all financial performance motivates everyone in their organization equally. This could not be further from the truth. Just as Maslow's hierarchy of needs identifies human performance to be a complex mix of basic and advanced desires and expectations, so is the corporate hierarchy. When organizations frame their strategic themes (i.e., what they are going to do with a strategy and how they are to execute it), they must acknowledge the mix between financial and nonfinancial objectives. Balance comes in the form of the careful, calculated sharing of financial and nonfinancial goals weaved into a strategy. We already know that people are motivated not only by money but also by the achievement of nonfinancial goals, which inherently lead to money.

A common misconception is that nonfinancial goals are non-numeric. That is also not true. Nonfinancial goals can be measured. Even perception can be measured, of course, with a level of inaccuracy. An engineering team discussing the balanced scorecard approach was very uncomfortable with the nonfinancial part of the equation because they believed that everything is measurable and the "foo-foo" (emotional) aspects of the program were irrelevant. The team leader, after acknowledging the perception, considered that a survey would be generated on how people felt about certain engineering results and that a perception index would be generated as a measure of improvement. The engineering team agreed whole-heartedly with the methodology.

Balance between Organizational Silos and the Overall Corporation   Organizations are challenged with what is the best business architecture for achieving the financial goals. Some believe that independent business units are best while others believe that corporate structures with centralized control are best. Others believe that certain key sustaining functions like human resources and information technology should be centralized to enable economies of scale and optimize resources, while others believe that each should be accountable for resources that they can control. These battles have been going on for centuries and we can see proof of any one of these architectures working. The U.S. Marine Corps has long been structured based on the basic business principles rather than business practices (i.e., that it wants independent thinkers on the front line who will have to be resourceful, and it wants strategic leadership from the top). Business principles should drive architecture rather than the other way around. Balanced scorecard can serve as a strong business principle. Balanced scorecard assists in the execution of a strategy and can be applied to any organizational structure and serves to provide the overriding clarity to strategic intent.

Balance of Finance with Operational Priorities   As long as business has been, finance is reputed for "bean counting" while operations made the beans. Centuries have evolved financial methods to accommodate to the evolution in business practice but one challenge still hinders business—the financial numbers do not reflect what truly goes on in business and hence strategy is difficult to measure and manage.

The change of business asset characteristics has exaggerated the challenge even further. In the past, the assets of a company would be reflected in the balance sheet but now 85 percent of the assets are intangible. Hence, the traditional financial statements measure only the tangible when the intangible is what fuels the future. A company could produce financial results through a core competency of garnering partnerships but this capability would not be reflected in the financial reports to shareholders. Of course, the obligatory annual report would declare this advantage in several well-photographed pictures of hands shaking in agreements. But this will not show competency.

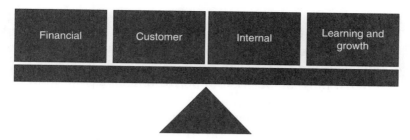

Exhibit 9.6   The Balance of Perspectives in Your Scorecard

Organizations that balance these competencies of financial measures of value to operational units are the ones that have placed analytical eyesight to their operational body. Exhibit 9.6 illustrates the balance among all the key performance measures and indicators that underlie the need for business transformation.

Four Perspectives of Balanced Scorecards   Professor Robert Kaplan and David Norton declare that strategy is a set of hypothesis about cause and effect in their first book *The Balanced Scorecard*.[26] Making strategy work in organizations demands that we take advantage and articulate strategy with several perspectives in mind to ensure that balance is maintained. Kaplan and Norton articulated four perspectives for review when articulating strategy in actionable terms. They did not specify that these perspectives are necessary and sufficient conditions for success. In fact, they recommend these perspectives but suggest that organizations add any perspectives that are more relevant. The perspectives are:

1. The financial perspective
   - What are the financial targets?
   - What drives these targets?
   - What kind of profit and revenue to achieve?
   - In a nonprofit, what budget guides you?
2. The customer perspective
   - Who are the customers?
   - How do you delight them?
   - What segments do you wish to address?
   - What goals do you wish to achieve with partners?
   - What are your goals for the distribution channel?

3. The internal perspective
   - Which processes must we be the best at to win customers?
   - What internal activities do we need to sustain competencies?
4. The learning and growth perspective
   - What must we be great in performing and how do we train our people to get up to that level?
   - What climate and culture nurtures growth?
   - What do we have to do in developing and training our people to achieve the other objectives?

These perspectives (see Exhibit 9.6) framed with an organization's mission, vision, values, and strategic themes form the balanced scorecard arsenal.

The Financial Perspective "What financial goals need to be achieved to realize your strategic themes and objectives?" In a profit-pursuing business, this financial perspective is the more overused and overdescribed or analyzed. The revenues, recurring and new, subscription-based or otherwise, margins and expenses are very important to an organization seeking to achieve its goals. Frankly, a common mistake with organizations is that they forget the link between the financial goals to the nonfinancial strategy of the company. The financial perspective gives respect to the relationship between stated financial goals and other goals that feed the machine to create the result.

It is important to note that in cause-driven organizations, like the U.S. Marine Corps or a nonprofit organization, the financial goal is not the most important overriding target that all other objectives feed into. It is really the mission that everything feeds into. Or in other cases, "In education, health, and not-for-profit organizations, service, not profit, is the defining characteristic."[27]

Given the profit-pursuing organizations, the financial perspective is critical as it forces recognition and definition to the main critical financial goals that the organization must achieve. Frankly, in these tough times, money may seem like everything but the financial perspective gives us the following reminders:

- The main goal of business is wealth-creation as measured by a series of financial targets achieved.
- The purpose of financial targets is to galvanize the operating units to manage performance and gain competencies for future success.

- It is one of many other perspectives but the one that funds the mission and purpose of the organization.
- It is a lagging indicator of performance because it records success not ahead of it.

The Customer Perspective "What customer-centric objectives must be achieved to attain your strategic themes?" This perspective is the second most forgotten or misunderstood set of objectives in business. Before setting goals using this perspective, answer the following questions:

- What is your target market?
- Who are/is your customer(s)?
- Who do they call our customers?
- Who do I compete against to gain the customer?
- What value does the existing customer of the organization perceive?
- If the organization disappeared, who would miss us? What will they do?

Often, the customers of today may not be the desired customers of tomorrow. As the audience of customers mature, what they desire in the organization changes also. What do your customers value?

Value, a term constantly used by marketing and business people, means many things to many people even as a definition. For the sake of fast learning, let us define *value proposition* as:

> Value proposition is the emotional, physical and symbolic residue derived by a customer once this individual or organization purchases the product or service for a price.

Often, the customer perspective is viewed as the set of objectives organizations must achieve to gain customer acquisition, acceptance, and perpetuation. These objectives are bounded or framed by the questions outlined earlier. Objectives are an outgrowth of assumptions made about the customers and their habits, the markets they represent, and the value they perceive in a relationship with your organization.

The Internal Perspective Companies seldom fail because they have the wrong strategy. They fail because they lack the methods to achieve the tactics that surround a strategy. The internal perspective reminds us that the background works, driven by objectives and goals, must be in place to ensure that the customer and financial objectives are achieved. Internal processes, mores, cultures, and procedures in all departments and business units support the value proposition to the target market segments. Typically, organizations have habits that are challenging to break or change in these perspectives. In other words, their internal behaviors will sabotage their ability to meet targets in the customer and the financial perspectives. These organizations must retool to win and this perspective helps them define what this retooling is. Conversely, if an organization can identify these internal characteristics and define ways to enable them, their execution arsenal can be tuned to win the customer, motivate the money, and also destroy the competition.

The Learning and Growth Perspective   Often laid off before people, training and development are the first to be removed from any shrinking budget. In crisis, the furthering of the capabilities of an organization is usually sacrificed. Organizations throughout history have behaved in short-term fashion, shrinking when times are tough and growing indiscriminately when times get better. This "inhale-exhale" methodology is what the learning and growth perspective serves to guard against. This perspective is the basis for all other perspectives and serves to remind the practitioner that the basis for all other results in the internal, customer, and financial perspectives is found in the learning and growth of the people. Learning, however, is not dictated by how you teach but by how people absorb new ideas and turn them into action. In a sense, it is more that just learning to action but the speed at which learning is transformed to action—a mean time between learning to action measure, so to speak. Often forgotten in strategy delivery systems, learning and growth form the foundation for the capabilities of the organization. Usually, current failure in the competitive business world is the result of past failures in the acknowledgement and exploitation of learning and the growth of talent.

Examples of learning and growth issues are:

- Training and development of key managers and would-be managers in certain skills
- Access to information among teams within various silos of the organization
- Employee satisfaction and motivation measures

Learning and growth, under this definition, are not the indeterminate activities found in various organizations. This is measurable and linked to the other productivity measures. In other words, this learning and growth measures for objectives are aligned to key deliverables in the other perspectives. Furthermore, this perspective reminds us of the relevance of continued learning and growth goals and how they affect the continued competitiveness of the organization.

Lean and Six Sigma

Lean gains its roots from the Toyota production system (TPS) and its primary focus is on learning to be both efficient and flexible. Focusing on seven forms of waste, lean has tremendous value to the business optimization process. Shigeo Shingo, one of the founders of the TPS, would often call conventional ideas like turning a nut onto a bolt waste because the final turn of the bolt is the most productive turn and the first correct placement of the nut on the tip of the bolt is the most productive also. He once "challenged workers on a job site to perform a dies exchange without turning any nut or bolt more than once. They had to pay me $500 for each extra turn!"[28]

Six Sigma should not be confused with lean as it is about developing a management strategy around the removal of variations and defects. Developed in Motorola and primarily defined for manufacturing business in the early years, it is now spreading across all industries.

Summary and Observations

There are two categories of performance management:

1. *Human performance management.* This category is about inspiring, organizing work, people performance, and incentives.
2. *Corporate performance management.* This is about analytics, tools, systems, and methods around the financial, operational, customer, and strategic outcomes and outputs of a corporation.

There are four elements to a performance platform that bring execution:

1. *Monitoring.* The art and science of observing and coaching employee activities and work.
2. *Measurement.* The art and science of gauging, using numbers and metrics and targets, how we are performing the tasks.
3. *Management.* The art and science of motivating, coaching, and enabling individuals and teams in the achievement of an objective.
4. *Direction setting.* The art and science of discovering strategic and tactical directions that are unique and differentiating in the marketplace, communicating this to all levels in the organization in the form that they can identify and corelate their day-to-day actions to goals.

Choosing Tools for a Performance Platform

How do we build and design an operating platform with tools that are really also management philosophies? Will they all collide? If each of these philosophies is the real reason the tools succeed, how do we combine them into the "unified" theory that makes a performance platform work? Is there a way to make it all seem to work together?

Ironically, there are many unifying theories. But these are really not impediments to an implementation. Any platform that you design functions on a common basis with the other if you can find a connection. Many are connected to each other through common definitions of processes or activities or elements of work. Hence you can build one on top or next to the other. Furthermore, trying to take all these tools into a unifying concept will only drown you in a heavy performance platform. The fundamental premise in a performance platform centers on processes, costs, and outcomes. The linkages to objectives and the strategic thrusts of the organization are a natural adjacency to this platform. Moving forward in designing the tool combination for such a platform begins with how you begin. If the organization is about processes, then begin there; if it is about costs, then start there.

Responding to Ambiguity and Agility Demands

The fundamentals of being an operational platform are based on predictability, scalability, maintainability, and measurability. Yet the new thought strategies focus on flexibility, the exception being the new rules, tipping points, transformation, and multiple inputs to transforming markets. One seems deterministic while the other wants determinism today but agility for tomorrow. How can a manufacturer become a service-based organization over time? Is that what organizations of the future behaved like with transformation occurring? If so, how do we design an operating performance platform for such major transformation? Strategic business design is about eyesight, foresight, and, most of all, insight into the 5- to 10-year horizon. It is not about changing on a dime. But part of the transformation is surviving today and hence investments are needed today. So how do we manage the demands of today as well as redesign for tomorrow?

Building the Plane While Flying the Plane?

I coined this phrase in 2003 because it gave me the real gut-level impressions of the danger of such a strategic direction. You have only one plane but if you just kept flying this plane, it would eventually encounter a storm that it cannot survive. If you stopped and built the place of the future, you would lose the battles you currently face. So, you must build a new plane while flying the plane into battle.

We seldom have the luxury of starting from scratch (i.e., from the ground up). But we have to build for tomorrow with the assets that are deployed for today. In programming, we learned to break a problem into logical parts, decomposing them into finite objects of deliver and input and work. Then we defined and designed them well. The same is true for strategy and execution of objectives. Invariably, certain parts of the design will require an agile approach, repeating, prototyping, trying, experimenting. This is somewhat nonlinear in its approach. Other portions may lend themselves to linear, time-based, predictable management. Both are strong approaches.

The challenge comes in investment—how much emphasis and dollars do you place on the current and the future when the current may not build for the future because the future is a transformed environment with different attributes? Prioritization is key here and many times the real challenge comes down to which part or side do you mortgage for the other. The science of this approach has been mastered like zero-based budgeting, business case creation and presentation, return of investment analysis, internal rate of returns, and the like. The art of decision prioritization on deciding on the right things to invest today and for tomorrow is what leaders are made of and frankly, get paid to do well.

The other challenge is that the focus on the transformation in the markets years from now could take your focus off the problems of just getting the business you want today to survive until the transformation occurs. You could be ahead of your time if you mistimed the market transformation.

Notes

1   Peter M. Senge, *The Fifth Discipline: The Art & Practice of The Learning Organization* (New York: Doubleday Currency, 1993).
2   Stephen R. Covey, *The 7 Habits of Highly Effective People* (New York: Simon & Schuster, 1990).
3   Vinay Couto, Frank Ribeiro, and Andrew Tipping, "It Makes Sense to Adjust," *Strategy and Business*, Issue 59, Summer 2010, May 25, 2010, p. 12.
4   Scott Martin, "More Companies Put iPads to Work," February 28, 2011, www.usatoday.com/tech/products/2011-02-28-ipad-enterprise_N.htm.
5   Steven Spear and H. Kent Bowen, "Decoding the DNA of the Toyota Production System," *Harvard Business Review*, September–October 1999.
6   Michael Hammer and James Champy, *Reengineering the Corporation: A Manifesto for Business Revolution* (New York: HarperBusiness, 1993).
7   Some treatment of the topic can also be found in Jeffrey G. Miller and Thomas E. Vollmann, "The Hidden Factory," *Harvard Business Review*, September–October 1985.
8   Norm Raffish and Peter B. B. Turney, ed., "The CAM-I Glossary of Activity-Based Management, version 1.2," Arlington, TX: The Consortium for Advanced Manufacturing—International, 1992.
9   H. Thomas Johnson and Robert S. Kaplan, *Relevance Lost: The Rise and Fall of Management Accounting* (Boston: Harvard Business Press, 1991).
10 John A. Miller, *Implementing Activity-Based Management in Daily Operations* (Hoboken, NJ: John Wiley & Sons, 1995).
11 Michael R. Ostrenga, Terrence R. Ozan, Robert D. McIlhattan, and Marcus D. Harwood, *The Ernst & Young Guide to Total Cost Management* (Hoboken, NJ: John Wiley & Sons, 1992).

12 Mohan Nair, *Activity-based Information Systems: An Executive's Guide to Implementation* (Hoboken, NJ: John Wiley & Sons, 1999).

13 Christopher Meyer, "How the Right Measures Help Teams Excel," *Harvard Business Review,* May–June 1994, p. 95.

14 Gary H. Anthes, "The Long Arm of Moore's Law," *Computerworld,* October 14, 1998, p. 69. Gordon Moore is cofounder of Intel Corporation. He identified this theory, which is used extensively to identify the growth of semiconductor complexity.

15 Faye A. Borthick and Harold Roth, "Faster Access to More Information for Better Decisions," *Journal of Cost Management,* Winter 1997, p. 25.

16 Peter Drucker presented this notion in his keynote speech at the Annual Users Group meeting for Cognos Corporation in 1997.

17 David Birchall and Laurence Lyons, "Creating Tomorrow's Organization: Unlocking the Benefits of Future Work," *Financial Times,* August 9, 1995, pp. 7–9. "A gap existed between the needs of the business and the capabilities of technology. Today all that has changed. The capabilities of information technology now outstrip the needs of business."

18 Vijay Govindarajan and Chris Trimble, *The Other Side of Innovation: Solving the Execution Challenge* (Boston: Harvard Business Press, 2010), p. 110.

19 Portions of this section are adapted from Mohan Nair, *Activity-Based Information Systems: An Executive's Guide to Implementation* (Hoboken, NJ: John Wiley & Sons, 1999).

20 Peter F. Drucker, "The Information Executives Truly Need," *Harvard Business Review,* January–February 1995, pp. 54–62.

21 John O. Whitney, "Strategic Renewal for Business Units," *Harvard Business Review,* July–August 1996, p. 85.

22 John Purcell, Nicholas Kinnie, Juani Swart, Bruce Rayton, and Susan Hutchinson, *People Management and Performance,* September 2008, pp. 31–33.

23 Mohan Nair, "Overcoming the 9 Deadly Sins of Balanced Scorecards," *The Journal of Corporate Accounting and Finance,* Volume 20, Issue 6, August 20, 2009, pp. 83–90. Here we describe how the balanced scorecard was implemented at Regence, a Blue Cross Blue Shield affiliate in the Pacific Northwest.

24 Peter F. Drucker, *Managing in a Time of Great Change* (Boston: Harvard Business Press, 2009), p. 118.

25 Douglas K. Smith, *Make Success Measurable! A Mindbook-Workbook for Setting Goals and Taking Action* (Hoboken, NJ: John Wiley & Sons, 1999), p. 14.

26   Robert S. Kaplan and David P. Norton, *The Balanced Scorecard: Translating Strategy into Action* (Boston: Harvard Business Press, 1996).

27   Howard Armitage and Cam Scholey, "Mapping Mavens: How Private and Public Companies Gain from Strategic Mapping," *CMA Management,* May 2003, pp. 15–18.

28   Shigeo Shingo (Translated by Andrew P. Dillon), *A Study of the Toyota Production System* (New York: Productivity Press, 1989), p. 109.

CHAPTER 10

Tales of Transformation

This chapter provides stories and examples of business transformation. These companies were not taken through this methodology or framework and are only examples for your review. The companies were not asked nor did they endorse this framework. However, they are companies that seem to fit the framework discussed in this book.

TriQuint Semiconductor

TriQuint Semiconductor, based in Beaverton, Oregon:

> ... designs, develops and manufactures advanced high-performance RF [radio frequency] solutions incorporating Gallium Arsenide (GaAs), Gallium Nitride (GaN), Surface Acoustic Wave (SAW) and Bulk Acoustic Wave (BAW) technologies for customers worldwide.[1]

They lead in a diverse set of products that fit into both the commercial and defense markets including smart phones, tablets, radar, and communications infrastructure applications. They live in the world of radio frequency. Their slogan is "Connecting the Digital World to the Global Network."

Understanding the New Principles of Transformation

Apart from the lower-order value of providing innovative technological advances in RF, a large component of their business is the intellectual, emotional, physical, and spiritual balance of his leaders and team. By spiritual, they mean a strong sense of community and connectedness are key to leadership. They make a keen connection between wellness and core purpose. Their work style is also about work purpose.

Transformation Scorecard[2]

Cause

- According to Triquint's CEO, Ralph Quinsey, the core purpose of the leadership team is to build a company for which they are proud, have a meaningful impact on stakeholders (customers, employees, investors, suppliers, and the communities where they work and live), and be a force for positive change.

Momentum Drivers They Serve

- The RF world is highly populated, but TriQuint continues to weather the transformation of this market. The team believes their broad and diverse offerings allow for innovative integrated solutions for their customers. The momentum in this market is driven by innovation to improve the experience of a virtual connection.

Core Competency

- What is their unique set of activities and processes that customers value above others? Apart from the lower-order value of providing innovative technological advances in RF, a large component of their business is the intellectual, emotional, physical, and spiritual balance of their leaders and team.

High-Order Value Proposition

- Their main theme in Triquint's products is to help their customers connect.

Starbucks

Howard Schultz, the leader of the new coffee industry, declares that Starbucks had two parents:

One is the original Starbucks, founded in 1971, a company passionately committed to world-class coffee and dedicated to educating its customers, one on one, about what great coffee can be. The other is the vision and values I brought to the company: the combination of competitive drive and a profound desire to make sure everyone in the organization could win together.[3]

The cause lives on and guides Starbucks' success. This attitude toward employees has been the foundation of its strategy and hence falls in the category of insight. Starbucks has operationalized its value proposition by establishing a culture of service within its own employees first. Starbucks knew what matters to the custodians of service, their employees, and knew that they would reflect servant leadership if they were served the servant leadership way.

Understanding the Principles of Transformation

I propose that Mr. Schultz did not franchise his business from the start because his cause was about everyone winning. His framework was built on a people business, not the coffee business. His insight was about a cultural transformation rather than an economic transformation, and yet both occurred. It seems that he wished for a world-class company that did not leave its people behind, and he stayed to his values. That became the Starbucks brand. People now speak of Starbucks less about its coffee and more about the reinvention of customer experience. The servant leadership principles that Starbucks was founded on started first within its walls. These principles are not about how employees lead one another but more about how they believe they must serve and lead their customers. After all, they are led the same way. Starbucks developed its operating principles in a pocket book called the "green apron book." This book speaks of "five ways of being":[4]

1. Be welcoming.
2. Be genuine.
3. Be considerate.
4. Be knowledgeable.
5. Be involved.

Starbucks, under the greatness of leadership and strategic insight, has formed new communities and a culture of connectedness. It has consciously built a foundation for community transformation as well as the transformation and creation of a new coffee culture. Now Starbucks sells many items in its retail outlets, but its workers never forget that they are serving first, selling second.

Transformation Scorecard[5]

Cause

- Serving the greater good of people both employees and customers.

Momentum

- People need a sense of community but also need to be private. A sense of community yet individuality.

Value

- *High-order*—community with people serving coffee to people. Validation that I am acknowledged.
- *Low-order*—good and personalized coffee.

Competencies

- Personalization with coffee.
- The ability to produce good coffee consistently with a strong relationship of the customer need.

Southwest Airlines

Everyone knows Southwest Airlines. So a description would be inappropriate but a good description of the nature and dynamism of this airline can be found in the work of Michael Porter in his *Harvard Business Review* article on strategy:[6]

> Their flight attendants are experts in all the required safety procedures but safety is not the point of their work. Fun is the point.[7]

The combination of activities permits Southwest Airlines to deliver on-time, low-cost, and point-to-point capability. Attendants are empowered. They clean the airplane if they have to, they ticket, they serve drinks, and they attend to the passengers rather than control the relationship of the people with the plane. This is reaffirmed by W. Chan Kim and Renee Mauborgne:

> Southwest Airlines created a blue ocean by breaking the trade-offs customers had to make between the speed of the airplanes and the economy and flexibility of car transport. To achieve this, Southwest offered high-speed transport with frequent and flexible departures at prices attractive to the mass of buyers. By eliminating and reducing certain factors of competition and raising others in the traditional airline industry, as well as by creating new factors drawn from the alternative industry of car transport, Southwest Airlines was able to offer unprecedented utility for airline travelers and achieve a leap in value with a low-end model.[8]

Understanding the New Principles of Transformation

People often don't fly, because it is a hassle. They don't like bags. They don't like being late. It is not fun anymore. It is too expensive and they can't rely on being treated equitably.

Some fly long hauls but many want to fly short hauls (i.e., point to point). Customers are cost sensitive, looking for efficiency, and they will give up comforts and choice for these.

This is the insight that makes the Southwest Airlines cabin different in experience. Michael Porter, a professor at Harvard University, stated in his seminal work "What Is Strategy?" that the essence of strategy is choosing to perform activities differently from the way rivals do. Porter states:

> Southwest's strategy involves a whole system of activities, not a collection of parts, its competitive advantage comes from the way its activities fit and reinforce one another.[9]

While competitive airlines developed sophisticated policies and procedures to give passengers safety in travel, Southwest conquered its high-order value proposition of safety through humor while making safety an assumption in the low-order value because they got passengers anywhere on time and for the right price.

Transformation Scorecard[10]

Cause

- Let anyone fly who wants to. Herb Kelleher, famed icon from Southwest Airlines, drove a new operational model for the airline industry but went beyond this to create an airline that symbolizes fun and cost consciousness. High spirit and low cost seems to be Southwest's motto. How did he operationally align this inspired message so that all employees got the message and made it their own? In giving people who could not travel a chance to travel, he "inspired our people to buy into a concept, to share a feeling and an attitude, to identify with the company—and then to execute."[11]

Market Momentum

- Time flies when you are having fun.
- Saving money is fun.

Customers Are

- Those who fly short hauls. Those who are willing to sacrifice their usual expectations for efficiency and cost (i.e., your own seat number, priority boarding, or bags).

Value Proposition

- *High-order value proposition*—A symbol of fun and freedom.
- *Low-order value proposition*—Low-cost and on time with warmth, friendliness, individual pride, and company spirit.

Partnerships Are

- The employees, unions, and airports. The airline defined a new way to work with unions in permitting crews to perform more than the usual tasks for the airplane.

Competencies[12]

- Limited passenger seating and service
- Frequent departure and short hauls (point-to-point)
- Productive ground and gate crews
- High aircraft usage
- Cost management (i.e., using one airplane model for consistency, driving down costs that the customer can see in the way they work and not just the price of the ticket).

Competition

- Long-haul players
- Low-fare, high-frequency players
- Hub-and-spoke airlines

Seldom-Known Facts about Southwest Airlines

Southwest Airlines first began catering to the male executive who wanted to fly point-to-point short haul business trips. They had only one business class, and it was the entire seat arrangement on the plane. Flight attendants, all female, wore short pants and were the prime attraction in the early years. They transformed as the market transformed from that customer target and value to other momentum drivers.

Southwest is the upstart airline and has always made fun of the way things are with other airlines. Its employees display a warrior spirit with efficiency and strive for the highest quality of service.

Les Schwab Tires

If you drive to a gasoline station in the western United States and tell them you may have a leak in your tire, they will most likely refer you to the nearest Les Schwab tire center if there is one near you. When you arrive at the center, two members of the center probably run to your car.[13] They may ask you what the problem is and almost throw you out of your car in an attempt to get you going. While you wait, you will be around tires that you may consider purchasing. You may sit concentrating on how much it may cost you to fix a leak. After a few moments, a Les Schwab employee will probably run to you or call your name and explain the problem. In this context, he or she would describe the issues and how his or her team solved the problem if it is a leak. Let us assume that he or she had removed a nail and patched the hole. You are surprised, because they could have sold you a tire but didn't. When you ask them what you owe them for their excellent service, he or she would probably say no problem; when you consider buying a tire, please come back again.

Les Schwab was an entrepreneur who transformed a tire shop into a multi-billion-dollar enterprise that became the largest independent tire store in the country.[14] The company employs about 7,000 employees at more than 20 stores and sells 6 million truck and car tires annually.

Understanding the New Principles of Transformation

He called his brand of customer service "sudden service."[15] Les Schwab tire centers were the first to bring together the sales offices and the retail products in the same location. He was the first, in 1954, to create the supermarket concept where the showroom and the warehouse were one.

The company would hand out free beef with the holiday spirit and gain the trust and loyalty of its customers. Les Schwab would appear in the advertisements with his characteristic hat. He seemed to breed loyalty because he would hire people who wanted to create businesses. Born poor, an orphan at age 15, Schwab learned early the value of hard work. He was raised by his uncle and aunt and delivered newspapers to pay for his boarding. With borrowed money and selling his house, he purchased the O.K. Rubber Welders tire franchise.

Transformational Scorecard[16]

Cause

- Sudden service by owners who are providing a service and building a high-integrity service to community.

Momentum

- People want service beyond tires.
- Trust is currency.

Value Proposition

- *High-order*—a community asset selling trust as the product
- *Low-order*—good tire service

Core Competency

- Fast retail delivery capability—their tires are at the store, they work immediately to serve you, and they are not a hard sell but a service-oriented shop.
- Good tires at a good price
- Fast service team
- Strong brand

Customer

- People who value speed, detail, tires, and trust

Partnerships

- His employees are running their own business. A profit-sharing plan is motivating for store managers.[17] Les builds an image by promoting from within, and that keeps the financial motivations and loyalty up.

Competition

- Costco, gas stations, Sears tire centers, and others

Markets in Transformation or Ready for Transformation

Many industries are showing the signs of transformation or transforming. This section highlights a few that might be of use in studying. Many more like health care and remote and mobile technology applications are moving fast in transformation as well.

Energy: Transforming Today

The energy markets have moved sideways with an emphasis on natural fuels. From biomass to forest health, the markets still dominated by traditional fuel sources are now moving to alternative sources of fuel. Diversification is the mantra of almost all the large energy companies. The market momentum has driven companies in these markets to reestablish their investments to reflect a respect of the environment and for the desires of the general community to take hold.

Markets shifted, first triggered by the fluctuating cost of oil, then by the devastations of oil spills. The public witnessed many disasters with regard to oil and its impacts to our environment, and the videos of sea creatures suffocating from what can be perceived as human indiscretion and greed turned the tide for commerce. It is not an issue of right and wrong, because many energy companies spend significant dollars on conservation and are also not to be held to one assumption because they are a diverse group of people who also care about our economy and our environment. It is ironic that we still consume more oil than others; we are not energy neutral in our consumption but we blame others. New markets for carbon credits and the like have emerged, and now the transformation of these markets is beginning.

Wind, solar, and other "natural" energy sources are being tapped as the future. Electric-powered cars, which once were viewed as ineffective vehicles, are now status symbols while the fast sports cars seem indulgences in this economic environment.

The momentum drivers for this transformation were the strong desire to save our planet from extinction and the moral obligation to protect the future for generations to come.

Consumers who valued gasoline for their car behaved like realized substance abusers who know they depend on it but want to be independent of it. Value and price shifted where a segment of the consumer base was willing to pay more for this belief while others remained strong to the current. The key driver, which is now no longer a trend but a momentum, is that a portion of the population wants to eliminate their personal items rather than accumulate.

Meanwhile, new dollars are being focused on clean technology markets. Just like companies that manufacture and market alcoholic beverages remind us to drink responsibly, energy companies remind us to consume with respect for our planet.

Like all transformations, the industry and the consumers are all in transition. They are trying to map the future while dealing with the present and what goes up may not go down. As I write this book, Libya is in chaos with the leaders of this country cracking down on its revolution. This has caused a rise in oil prices that was not predicted before this event but is the impact of a population of people seeking their own freedom. Such unknown unknowns happen frequently in transformational markets and will exaggerate the desire for alternative fuel sources.

Higher Education: Transforming Soon

Peter Drucker, the father of modern management, wrote, "And what about the large university? The costs of higher education in all developed countries are nearly as out of control as the costs of healthcare."[18]

As discussed earlier, the higher education market indicates all the signs of a pending strategic transformation. This market is ripe for significant transformation because the market pricing of these universities combined with the consumer outrage is colliding. There are no jobs to feed the educated, and this will bring with it the outrage of the silent contract between the institutions and graduates, which is that if they went to college, took out loans, and were willing to pay them back, it must be because they will be hired when they are done.

In June 2010, for the first time in history, student loan debt surpassed credit card debt in the United States. This means that people will pay off their credit cards before their student loans. This also means that the institutions that give loans are lenders of learning but want their cash back at some point. Combine this challenge with the double-digit unemployment numbers in various states, and we can see that the triggers for transformation start to form a potent force.

Consumers do not really know the value of their education. Depending on the economy and the job market, graduates could earn more than when they entered the university system or they could not be able to find work. But the days of getting a better job because of attaining higher education seem to be over, except in India, China, and Brazil, to mention a few fast-moving nations. The Ivy League schools have reputations and strong brand power to attract and retain their applicants and receive donations and grants. Research grants, donations, and a great sports program all add to the financial machinery, but what if the alumni can't find work that they prefer?

The institutions view themselves as destinations, and this has worked well when the alumni identify themselves with the institution and maybe the football team, for example. Institutions that hold onto their alumni and gather a following can survive and grow only if their alumni are employed. The institutions after transformation must believe themselves to be way stations, not destinations, and must build up the competence to teach and create workers with a differentiating value to society.

We find many segments that will compete in battle for identity. For example:

- Ivy League schools
- State schools
- Independent liberal arts schools
- Overseas schools connected to U.S.-based schools
- Not-for-profit schools
- For-profit schools
- Faith-based schools

What is the impact of joblessness to the U.S. educational ecosystem? What will be the response by the institutions that are mostly enjoying the increase in applicants currently and may lull themselves into believing that it is the brand or the need for education that is driving this phenomenon? What is the impact of the globalization of education and the use of ubiquitous technologies that can allow for entrants to function in a school but not be at the schools?

A student who cannot find work in the United States may choose a school in India to acculturate herself while studying to receive a degree. For example, consider Great Lakes University in Chennai, India. Students pursue an MBA with world-class educators from all over the United States and the world. And they are expected to perform service to the community as a requirement of graduation. The business school has partnerships with Yale and the University of Houston to mention a few. Furthermore, the chairman of the university, Professor Bala Balachandran, sees it as his responsibility to place his graduates in jobs. In the United States, the universities offer good value but international competition is increasing. The public is fast realizing that the price must be paid back through some job that they will have to take. We are also sending messages to many that a degree is our destiny and this, even though noble, will stress the system. Not all institutions will need to worry. But who that is remains a mystery.

What should the institutions do with regard to transformation of their industry? If anyone wants to see classes in progress, they can pull up iTunesU or Google and catch a class. Access seems less an issue in the future, and educators don't need to talk about books because students can download them instantaneously. The knowledge in textbooks, if accessible, makes them obsolete. Classrooms and professors' presentations are also getting on-line. So, we can experience the lesson from far away, making the real asset of an education not the information transferred or the data but the wisdom from the teachers and the other students.

Institutions can consider value as the following:

- Consider job-creating competencies from entrepreneurship to internships and job placements.
- Align hiring organizations with projects and partnerships.
- Align government beyond negotiating subsidies to actual plans and partnerships to create opportunities.

- Be humble and less concerned about brand and more about students and how they express the brand in their daily work as alumni.
- Create a set of partnerships that allow transfers between schools so that a school does not need to be good at everything. Share competence and create a collection.
- Engage the local community and be a community asset (e.g., one university shares its library with the community so that the value is reciprocated).
- Rethink the model that to go to school, students must leave their work because they may not want to lose the opportunity they have.

The Internet has transformed education. George Fox University in Newberg, Oregon, envisions itself to have a virtual library because the personal library will be on laptops or iPads that students carry with them. We have seen the demise of physical library research because we can find anything from anywhere from our keyboard. This disruptive technology has in a few years transformed the classroom setting into a virtual platform. Collaborations can occur globally at any time, and we live as much in the virtual universe as we are in the real one.

Recently I was asked to teach a class at a local university. I arrived thinking that I would have young attentive students before me hanging on every word. The class was small and the number of students was large but scattered all across the state and beyond via video feed. The majority of the students who were in front of me did not look at me but for a moment. They were peering at their laptops, taking notes on their laptops, downloading articles, and occasionally checking to see whether I was still standing. Furthermore, I learned that they meet only irregularly and the rest of the lessons are via the Internet, where the dialog is rich, ubiquitous, asynchronous, and highly productive.

The financing model, the educational delivery model, the learning model, and the access model are all changing at the same time in higher education. With the influx of global alternatives, the acceleration of educational transformation is eminent. Parents must save all their working lives to serve their children in education. The students must get loans while the educational institutions seek endowments to grow. The brand promise of a better life after education is fading combined with for-profit entrants disrupting the comfortable view that universities are community assets in many of our minds. All these issues collide to form the motivation for strategic business transformation.

Notes

1   Triquint Semiconductor. www.triquint.com/company/index.cfm.
2   This approach is assembled by the author. It is used as an example and should not be assumed to be TriQuint's transformation strategy.
3   Howard Schultz, *Pour Your Heart into It: How Starbucks Built a Company One Cup at a Time* (New York: Hyperion, 1999), p. 11.
4   Joseph A. Michelli, *The Starbucks Experience: 5 Principles for Turning Ordinary into Extraordinary* (New York: McGraw-Hill, 2006), pp. 20–21.
5   This approach is assembled by the author and is not from Starbucks. It is used as an example and should not be assumed to be Starbucks' strategy.
6   Michael E. Porter, "What Is Strategy?" *Harvard Business Review,* November 1, 1996, pp. 61–78.
7   James M. Kouzes and Barry Z. Posner, *Encouraging the Heart: A Leader's Guide to Rewarding and Recognizing Others* (San Francisco: Jossey-Bass, 2003), p. 134.
8   W. Chan Kim and Renee Mauborgne, *Blue Ocean Strategy: How to Create Uncontested Market Space and Make Competition Irrelevant* (Boston: Harvard Business Press, 2005), p. 38.
9   "What is strategy?" *Harvard Business Review,* Nov-Dec 1996. www.ipocongress.ru/download/guide/article/what_is_strategy.pdf.
10   This approach is assembled by the author and is not from Southwest Airlines. It is used as an example and should not be assumed to be Southwest's strategy.
11   Frances Hesselbein and Paul M. Cohen, *Leader to Leader: Enduring Insights on Leadership from the Drucker Foundation's Award-Winning Journal* (San Francisco: Jossey-Bass, 1999), p. 47.
12   Porter, "What Is Strategy?" pp. 61–78.
13   "Les Schwab, Who Turned a Rundown Shop Into a Tire Chain, Dies at 89." *The New York Times.* www.nytimes.com/2007/06/10/business/10schwab.html?_r=1&fta=y.
14   "The tire king: Les Schwab at 80." Oregon Live.com. http://blog.oregonlive.com/oregonianextra/1997/09/profile_of_les_schwab_in_1997.html.
15   Tires Les Schwab. www.lesschwab.com/lsdifference.asp.
16   This approach is assembled by the author and is not from Les Schwab. It is used as an example and should not be assumed to be Les Schwab's strategy.

17 "But the rubber truly meets the road with a generous profit-sharing plan that allows even hourly workers to reap rewards from their store's success. Half of store profits are set aside for bonuses, health benefits, and retirement trusts. It's not unusual for store managers to earn six figures and retire as millionaires." www.fastcompany.com/magazine/74/beef.html.

18 Peter F. Drucker, *Managing for the Future* (New York: Butterworth-Heinemann, 1993), p. 129.

Glossary

Activity-Based Cost/Management
An alternative to traditional accounting methods, providing an activity view of where overhead is assigned in businesses, reducing the general distortion often suffered. This model, introduced by Professors Robert S. Kaplan and H. Thomas Johnson, has grown to be an understood method for costing products and services in the Global 100.

Balanced Scorecard
A formalism, methodology, and framework that translates strategy to actionable and measureable objectives. Following four perspectives, balanced scorecard (BSC) balances these objectives among nonfinancial and financial, leading and lagging, operations, and finance. This methodology allows for all parts of the organization to know and understand their contribution to strategy.

Cascading the Scorecard
The action of driving objectives, measures, targets, and initiatives into the organization and through multiple levels.

Cause
The core purpose of the organization. A greater goal that is taken rather than given by all employees. A cause transforms your customers but also transforms the organization.

Cause and Effect
The effect of recognizing the relationship among strategic themes and their influence on one another.

Champion
A person who is tasked or has taken the role of motivating, articulating change, and organizing business transformation.

Capability
The set of activities that the organization performs well.

Core Competency
The basic set of capabilities and habits a corporation has that is unique to its personality and skills. Competency is a recipe of your activities that you align to the differentiating value proposition you offer the target customers.

Data Obesity
A phenomenon in which organizations are inundated with data at all levels and cannot use it or understand its value.

Fox
The individual influencing the target customer.

High-Order Value Proposition
The symbolic value of purchasing a product or a service.

Information Starved
A phenomenon in which organizations are unable to discover relevance in the information they have to work with.

Initiatives
The key programs an organization must undertake to enable objectives to be achieved. Some take the form of change programs like ISO 9000 or leadership training.

Key Performance Indicators
Known in the industry as essential measures that are critical for strategic or tactical realization.

Lagging Indicator
A measure(s) that is identified only after an event occurs.

Leading Indicator
A measure(s) that can indicate the result of an event prior to it occurring.

Learning Adoption Cycle
The process of moving an organization through four phases:

1. *Trigger phase*—an event that forces everyone to take a second look at solving problems.
2. *Education phase*—the process of learning of solutions to the existing problems to answer the question "what is it?"
3. *Pilot phase*—the process of testing the solution in a small unit or section of the organization to answer the question "does it work for me?"
4. *Production phase*—the process of moving into a sustainable enterprise model with the question "can it work continuously?"

Low-Order Value Proposition
The rational and the emotional value derived from purchasing your product or service.

Measure
A quantifiable formula whose variables define what needs to be measured and monitored for a target to be achieved.

Mission
The charge given to an organization to act upon.

Momentum
The movement of prospects of mass, the desire to purchase product/service with velocity.

Momentum Driver
Forces that influence momentum.

Objective
A goal that is specific, measurable, and actionable and ends in a desired result in a specific time frame.

Operational Excellence
Doing an activity well.

Performance Measure
The methods to align performance results to measures and to manage this process.

Performance Measure Dictionary
A document that collects, describes, and manages all the descriptions and connections in a set of measures of performance of a corporation.

Performance Platform
There are three subsystems to this platform: people, technology, and process.

Perspectives
Balanced scorecard describes four main perspectives to consider in formulating strategic directions:

1. *Financial perspective*—key financial objectives that define the overall strategic themes achievement.
2. *Customer perspective*—issues of value, competency, and customer-related objectives.
3. *Internal perspective*—operational, channel, and group objectives that lead and support the financial and customer goals.
4. *Learning and growth perspective*—the objectives that feed all other perspectives as the foundation for mobilizing and sustaining the organization in strategy realization.

Strategic Business Transformation
The design of your business in transformative times, declaring what you stand for, who you consider the customers, and what you do well compared to others.

Strategic Paradox
The syndrome in which the management team of an organization believes that strategy is being executed in one fashion while the real activities of an organization are performed counter to or differently from the strategy.

Strategic Positioning
Performing similar activities differently while capturing customer attention and value.

Strategic Theme
Key strategic objectives for differentiation, focus, and market dominance.

Strategic Thrust
See *strategic theme.*

Strategic Variable
Key drivers and assumptions to strategy themes that, once changed, can affect the validity of the strategy.

Strategy Mapping
The process of linking all the strategic objectives within the four perspectives into a cause-and-effect map.

Target
A numeric or nonnumeric value representing a desired result.

Target Customer
The prospects that are most likely to purchase your products and services first. If you believe everyone is your customer, no one becomes your customer. Targeting a specific persona and customer type allows your organization to focus all activities to attract, retain, and delight this customer. It does not mean that you have only this target and forget others. It only means that this is your reference point.

Transformational Servant Leadership
Leadership based on servant leadership principles but become leaders through personal transformation and self discovery. Transformational servant leadership is about those leaders who find a cause greater than themselves. These leaders, through their discovery, develop their skills, plans, and vision to achieve the task. Transformational servant leaders are ones who also look to service as their first frame of reference and through service, they gather a following.

Trend
General direction of purchase or behavior.

Value Proposition
Usually associated with products and services, this is the emotional, symbolic, and practical residue after a customer envisions payment for a product or service.

Values
How an organization wishes to exist.

Vision
The sight of the mind. Organizational vision is the statement of what an organization sees as the state of the future.

Suggested Reading

Balanced Scorecard

Becker, Brian E., Mark A. Huselid, and David Ulrich. *The HR Scorecard: Linking People, Strategy, and Performance* (Boston: Harvard Business Press, 2001).

Kaplan, Robert S., and David P. Norton. *The Balanced Scorecard: Translating Strategy into Action* (Boston: Harvard Business Press, 1996).

Kaplan, Robert S., and David P. Norton. *The Strategy-Focused Organization: How Balanced Scorecard Companies Thrive in the New Business Environment* (Boston: Harvard Business Press, 2000).

Niven, Paul R. *Balanced Scorecard Step-by-Step for Government and Nonprofit Agencies, Second Edition* (Hoboken, NJ: John Wiley & Sons, 2008).

Niven, Paul R. *Balanced Scorecard Step-by-Step: Maximizing Performance and Maintaining Results, Second Edition* (Hoboken, NJ: John Wiley & Sons, 2006).

Activity-Based Cost/Management

Balachandran, Bala. "Cost Management at Saturn: A Case Study," *BusinessWeek Executive Briefing Services* Vol. 5, 1994, pp. 25–28.

Johnson, H. Thomas, and Robert S. Kaplan. *Relevance Lost: The Rise and Fall of Management Accounting* (Boston: Harvard Business Press, 1991).

Kaplan, Robert S., and Robin Cooper. *Cost & Effect: Using Integrated Cost Systems to Drive Profitability and Performance* (Boston: Harvard Business Press, 1997).

Nair, Mohan. *Activity-based Information Systems: An Executive's Guide to Implementation* (Hoboken, NJ: John Wiley & Sons, 1999).

Nair, Mohan. *Essentials of Balanced Scorecard* (Hoboken, NJ: John Wiley & Sons, 2004).

Strategy

Benioff, Marc, with Carlye Adler. *The Business of Changing the World: Twenty Great Leaders on Strategic Corporate Philanthropy* (New York: McGraw-Hill, 2006).

Christensen, Clayton M. *The Innovator's Dilemma: When New Technologies Cause Great Firms to Fail* (Boston: Harvard Business Press, 1997).

Hamel, Gary, and C. K. Prahalad. *Competing for the Future* (Boston: Harvard Business Press, 1996).

Hamel, Gary, and C. K. Prahalad. "Strategic Intent," *Harvard Business Review* (May–June 1989).

Kim, W. Chan, and Renee Mauborgne. *Blue Ocean Strategy: How to Create Uncontested Market Space and Make Competition Irrelevant* (Boston: Harvard Business Press, 2005).

Kim, W. Chan, and Renee Mauborgne. "Value Innovation: The Strategic Logic of High Growth," *Harvard Business Review* (January–February 1997).

Nair, Mohan. "How Causes Can Animate Companies," *Strategy and Business*, August 28, 2007, www.strategy-business.com/article/li00040.

Ohmae, Kenichi. "Getting Back to Strategy," *Harvard Business Review* (November–December 1988).

Porter, Michael E. *Competitive Advantage: Creating and Sustaining Superior Performance* (New York: Free Press, 1998).

Porter, Michael E. *Competitive Strategy: Techniques for Analyzing Industries and Competitors* (New York: Free Press, 1998).

Porter, Michael E. "What Is Strategy?" *Harvard Business Review* (November–December 1996), pp. 61–78.

Schiemann, William A., and John H. Lingle. "Seven Greatest Myths of Measurement," *Management Review* (May 1997), p. 29.

Slywotzky, Adrian J. *Value Migration: How to Think Several Moves Ahead of the Competition* (Boston: Harvard Business Press, 1995).

Business and Servant Leadership

Drucker, Peter F. *Managing for the Future* (New York: Butterworth-Heinemann, 1993).

Easwaran, Eknath. *Gandhi the Man* (Petaluma, CA: Nilgiri Press, 1972).

Gandhi, Rajmohan. *The Good Boatman: A Portrait of Gandhi* (India: Viking, 1995).

Greenleaf, Robert K. *The Servant-Leader Within: A Transformative Path* (New York: Paulist Press, 2003).

Greenleaf, Robert K. *The Power of Servant Leadership* (San Francisco: Berrett-Koehler Publishers, 1998).

Greenleaf, Robert K. (edited by Don M. Frick and Larry C. Spears). *On Becoming a Servant Leader: The Private Writings of Robert K. Greenleaf* (San Francisco: Jossey-Bass, 1996).

Hammerschlag, Carl A. *Theft of the Spirit: A Journey to Spiritual Healing* (New York: Simon & Schuster, 1970).

Hesselbein, Frances, and Paul M. Cohen. *Leader to Leader: Enduring Insights on Leadership from the Drucker Foundation's Award-Winning Journal* (San Francisco: Jossey-Bass, 1999).

Kouzes, James M., and Barry Z. Posner. *Encouraging the Heart: A Leader's Guide to Rewarding and Recognizing Others* (San Francisco: Jossey-Bass, 2003).

Krass, Peter. *The Book of Leadership Wisdom: Classic Writings by Legendary Business Leaders* (Hoboken, NJ: John Wiley & Sons, 1998).

Lencioni, Patrick. *The Five Dysfunctions of a Team: A Leadership Fable* (San Francisco: Jossey-Bass, 2002).

Mourkogiannis, Nikos. *Purpose: The Starting Point of Great Companies* (New York: Palgrave Macmillan, 2006).

Nair, Keshavan. *A Higher Standard of Leadership: Lessons from the Life of Gandhi* (San Francisco: Berrett-Koehler, 1997).

Nair, Mohan. "The Ten Deadly Sins of CEOs," *Journal of Accounting and Finance* (Hoboken: John Wiley & Sons, 2002), pp. 45–51.

Schultz, Howard. *Pour Your Heart into It: How Starbucks Built a Company One Cup at a Time* (New York: Hyperion, 1999).

Tulku, Tarthang. *Gesture of Balance: A Guide to Awareness, Self-Healing, and Meditation* (Berkeley: Dharma Press, 1977).

Innovation

Davila, Tony, Marc J. Epstein, and Robert Shelton. *Making Innovation Work: How to Manage It, Measure It, and Profit from It* (Upper Saddle River NJ: Prentice Hall, 2005).

Govindarajan, Vijay, and Chris Trimble. *10 Rules for Strategic Innovators: From Idea to Execution* (Boston: Harvard Business Press, 2005).

Govindarajan, Vijay, and Chris Trimble. *The Other Side of Innovation: Solving the Execution Challenge* (Boston: Harvard Business Press, 2010).

Johnson, Steven. *Where Good Ideas Come From: The Natural History of Innovation* (New York: Riverhead Books, 2010).

Kelley, Tom, with Jonathan Littman. *The Art of Innovation: Lessons in Creativity from IDEO, America's Leading Design Firm* (New York: Currency, 2001).

Michelli, Joseph A. *The Starbucks Experience: 5 Principles for Turning Ordinary into Extraordinary* (New York: McGraw-Hill, 2006).

About the Author

Mohan Nair brings a broad experience to business transformation as high-tech entrepreneur, educator, strategy consultant, and health-care executive. As chief innovation officer at a health plan in the Northwest/Mountain State region, Mohan leads a business incubation team focused on achieving a transformed health-care system.

Mohan founded Emerge Inc., a business advisory firm guiding clients challenged with business transformation. Mohan has been president of ABC Technologies, Inc., a leader in activity-based cost management software, now of SAS Corporation; and president/chief operating officer of Protools Inc., which was acquired. He has also served marketing and engineering roles in several established high-tech organizations as well.

For over 10 years, he served as an adjunct professor of business and management with the Kellogg School of Management, teaching executive courses in supply-chain management and cost/performance management. He authored two books, *An Executive's Guide to Activity-based Management Systems* and *Essentials of Balanced Scorecard* (John Wiley & Sons), and has authored articles in several noted journals and magazines, including the *Journal of Corporate Accounting*, the *Journal of Corporate Finance and Accounting*, and the *International Journal of Servant Leadership*. He has appeared on CNBC-Asia, *PM Magazine* in the United States, and Singapore Television as a cohost in a prime-time magazine program titled *In and Around*.

Mohan has served the nation in several capacities: as a member of the Armed Services Interest Group on Cost and Performance Management for the Consortium of Advanced Management International; as a member of the Government's Committee on Performance and Accountability for the State of Oregon; and he has been called by the U.S. Department of Health and Human Services to serve on the AHIC Chronic Care Workgroup.

He holds a BS and MS in Computer and Information Science at the University of Oregon and is an alumnus of the Advanced Management College at Stanford University. Mohan is currently the chairman of the Board of Trustees for the Oregon Independent College Foundation, and he is also a board member for the Big Brother Big Sister Association.

Index